PUFFIN BOOKS

I LIKE THIS POem

Kaye Webb became Editor of Puffin Books in 1961. During the 1960s and 1970s her instinct and flair resulted in the outstanding growth and development of Puffin, and in 1967 she launched the highly successful Puffin Club – now the Puffin Book Club. She was widely known for her remarkable contribution to children's books, and was awarded the MBE in 1974. She retired from Puffin in 1979, but remained heavily involved in the children's book world. Kaye Webb died in January 1996.

I LIKE THIS POem

A CLASSIC ANTHOLOGY TO TREASURE

EDITED BY KAYE WEBB

ILLUSTRATED BY ANTONY MAITLAND

PUFFIN

PUFFIN BOOKS

Published by the Penguin Group
Penguin Books Ltd, 80 Strand, London WC2R ORL, England
Penguin Group (USA) Inc., 375 Hudson Street, New York, New York 10014, USA
Penguin Group (Canada), 90 Eglinton Avenue East, Suite 700, Toronto, Ontario, Canada M4P 2Y3
(a division of Pearson Penguin Canada Inc.)
Penguin Ireland, 25 St Stephen's Green, Dublin 2, Ireland (a division of Penguin Books Ltd)
Penguin Group (Australia), 250 Camberwell Road, Camberwell, Victoria 3124, Australia
(a division of Pearson Australia Group Pty Ltd)
Penguin Books India Pvt Ltd, 11 Community Centre, Panchsheel Park, New Delhi – 110 017, India
Penguin Group (NZ), 67 Apollo Drive, Rosedale, North Shore 0632, New Zealand
(a division of Pearson New Zealand Ltd)
Penguin Books (South Africa) (Pty) Ltd, 24 Sturdee Avenue, Rosebank, Johannesburg 2196, South Africa

Penguin Books Ltd, Registered Offices: 80 Strand, London WC2R ORL, England

puffinbooks.com

First published 1979
46

Copyright © Puffin Club, 1979
Illustrations copyright © Antony Maitland, 1979
All rights reserved

The acknowledgements on pages 183–6 constitute an extension of this copyright page.

Set in Monotype Ehrhardt
Made and printed in England by Clays Ltd, St Ives plc

British Library Cataloguing in Publication Data
A CIP catalogue record for this book is available from the British Library

ISBN: 978-0-140-31295-9

A Note for Interested Adults

The exciting and, we believe, unique thing about this book is that it is the only collection of poems in existence chosen by children.

Poetry anthologies for young readers, while almost always imaginative and stimulating, can have one disadvantage – if disadvantage it be. They are put together by adults, who are limited not only by individual taste but sometimes by an inclination to leave out what is to them over-familiar.

This anthology is different, because the poems you will find here are winnowed from nearly 1,000 enthusiastic recommendations made by children themselves. Of course, many of the poems were submitted more than once, and in the case of the most popular poets, Robert Louis Stevenson, Walter de la Mare, A. A. Milne and Spike Milligan, I had to make a choice among poems with equal votes. Nine tenths of the book is made up of the poems or poets most often named. The remaining tenth are there because of their surprising freshness and to add spice to the whole. In general, what has emerged is a salutary reminder that we have to 'begin at the beginning', and that a poem which may have come to seem almost trite to a grown-up can mean an abrupt falling in love when it is encountered for the first time.

It might be argued that, coming from one particular group of children, the choices are not necessarily indicative of what all children like. But it should be noted that the poems submitted were distributed among more than eighty different anthologies, as well as nineteen books of collected poems and a generous handful of novels and school readers. A further point is that many schools of many kinds are represented, a good number from other parts of the world (a reason for some of the more unusual entries), so it seems safe to say that these poems are genuinely ones that all children are likely to enjoy at some time or other.

How were we to present such a mixed bag? It seemed that the best and most useful way would be to arrange the poems by age, since the divisions are generally so sharp.

We asked for reasons why a particular poem was chosen, and the enthusiasm which seemed to spring out at us from the lovingly written lines, often with charming illustrations, convinced us that these were genuine choices. Younger ages were charmed by 'funny words' and 'good rhythms'. They liked talking animals (cats, dogs, frogs, mice), and they also sent in a fair sprinkling of poems about the weather. Nine and ten year olds, while still susceptible to jokes and rhyme, went for more exotic animals, and were also more interested in people and places and a spot of action. (How could I have forgotten the excitement and sadness of 'The Charge of the Light Brigade' and my own delight and discovery of the marvellous freedom of 'Hiawatha', so easy to remember and imitate.) Disconcerting but nice to find that 'Night Mail' by W. H. Auden was chosen because '*it rhymes well and is easy to remember*', and disarming to be told that '*poems are usually boring but this one* ["The Marrog" by R. S. Scriven] *is not*'.

The eleven and twelve year old entries were more into feelings, hidden meanings and beautiful phrases. They were also discovering the newer poets: Charles Causley, Stevie Smith and Michael Rosen alongside John Betjeman and T. S. Eliot, and by the time we arrived at the thirteen, fourteen and fifteen year olds we had a good sprinkling of religion, philosophy and what might be called 'aids to living'. In fact the advocate of 'A Welsh Testament' by R. S. Thomas told us, '*When in need of courage it ought to be referred to.*'

Finally when (stunned by the glamour of the name) I read that Ballgobin Rehoutee's reason for recommending 'Reeds of Innocence' was that '*I at once thought of my childhood – at that time we didn't even know one problem existed*' – it seemed that the selection was complete.

Perhaps this book should really have been entitled *It Makes Me Happy*, because this was the reason most often given for sending the best-loved poems. Certainly putting it together has been a joyful affair for me; not only because of reviving old enthusiasms but because I believe it will give pleasure to all the children and adults who happen to come by it, and I know it will carry comfort to those other children who are currently deprived of material things as well as poetry. If it makes *them* a little happier, then everyone who has contributed to this book will be well rewarded.   KAYE WEBB (1979)

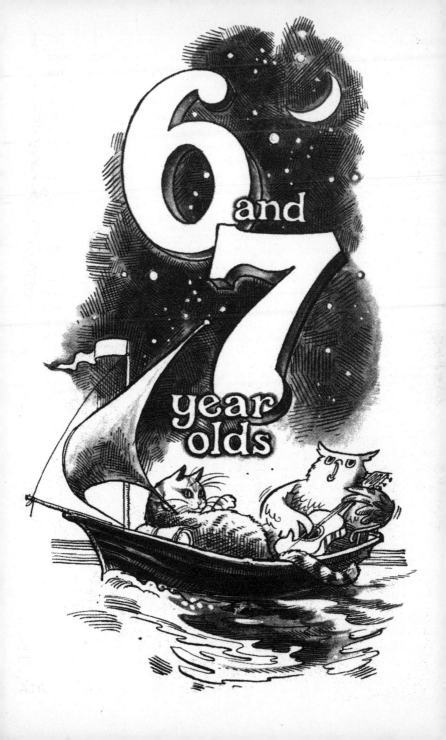

6 and 7 year olds

The Witches' Spell

Double, double, toil and trouble;
Fire burn, and cauldron bubble.
Fillet of a fenny snake
In the cauldron boil and bake;
Eye of newt, and toe of frog,
Wool of bat, and tongue of dog,
Adder's fork, and blind-worm's sting,
Lizard's leg and owlet's wing,
For a charm of powerful trouble,
Like a hell-broth, boil and bubble.
Double, double, toil and trouble;
Fire burn, and cauldron bubble.

WILLIAM SHAKESPEARE
(from *Macbeth*)

I like this poem because in the part 'fire burn, and cauldron bubble' it makes me think of volcanoes erupting. This poem is a spell. The hell-broth is the volcano's soup. Hell is under the ground, the hell-broth is coming from all naughty people who are making it. In the middle the witches put all the horrible ingredients.

The second 'fire burn, and cauldron bubble' is the volcano erupting again. 'Double, double' sounds like my soup boiling. 'Snake, bake' sounds like the fat in the frying-pan spitting. 'Frog, dog' sounds like Mummy's cake ingredients going thud in the bowl. 'Sting, wing' is the cooking starting to hum. The rhyming words sound like the cooking gaining energy. I think that everything the witches put in makes the spell stronger. MARIE HARBOUR

On the Ning Nang Nong

On the Ning Nang Nong
Where the Cows go Bong!
And the Monkeys all say Boo!
There's a Nong Nang Ning
Where the trees go Ping!
And the tea pots Jibber Jabber Joo.
On the Nong Ning Nang
All the mice go Clang!
And you just can't catch 'em when they do!
So it's Ning Nang Nong!
Cows go Bong!
Nong Nang Ning!
Trees go Ping!
Nong Ning Nang!
The mice go Clang!
What a noisy place to belong,
Is the Ning Nang Ning Nang Nong!!

SPIKE MILLIGAN

*... because the animals say different things to what they really say,
because cows really say 'moo' and not 'bong' and mice don't say 'clang'
they say 'squeak' and teapots don't really talk. This poem is very hard
to say because the 'nings' and 'nangs' and 'nongs' get mixed up and
my tongue gets in a twist.* DEBRA GRICE

The Owl and the Pussy-Cat

The Owl and the Pussy-Cat went to sea
   In a beautiful pea-green boat:
They took some honey, and plenty of money
   Wrapped up in a five-pound note.
The Owl looked up to the stars above,
   And sang to a small guitar,
'O lovely Pussy, O Pussy, my love,
   What a beautiful Pussy you are,
           You are,
           You are!
   What a beautiful Pussy you are!'

Pussy said to the Owl, 'You elegant fowl,
   How charmingly sweet you sing!
Oh! let us be married; too long we have tarried
   But what shall we do for a ring?'
They sailed away, for a year and a day,
   To the land where the bong-tree grows;
And there in a wood a Piggy-wig stood,
   With a ring at the end of his nose,
           His nose,
           His nose,
   With a ring at the end of his nose.

'Dear Pig, are you willing to sell for one shilling
   Your ring?' Said the Piggy, 'I will.'
So they took it away, and were married next day
   By the turkey who lives on the hill.
They dined on mince and slices of quince,

Which they ate with a runcible spoon;
And hand in hand, on the edge of the sand,
They danced by the light of the moon,
    The moon,
    The moon,
They danced by the light of the moon.

EDWARD LEAR

... because I like owls and pussy-cats and they are acting like people. I like to think of them doing the things in the poem. It is a happy poem and it always makes me feel happy. URSULA ROBERTS

The Tickle Rhyme

'Who's that tickling my back?' said the wall.
'Me,' said a small
Caterpillar. 'I'm learning
To crawl!'

IAN SERRAILLIER

... because I think it is a very funny poem because it tickles me and my family and I expect it will tickle you too when you read it.
SUSANNE THOMAS

Windy Nights

Whenever the moon and stars are set,
    Whenever the wind is high,
All night long in the dark and wet,
    A man goes riding by.
Late in the night when the fires are out,
Why does he gallop and gallop about?

Whenever the trees are crying aloud,
    And ships are tossed at sea,
By, on the highway, low and loud,
    By at the gallop goes he.
By at the gallop he goes, and then
By he comes back at the gallop again.

ROBERT LOUIS STEVENSON

... because it makes me think of night-time and helps me to go to sleep, and because I like to think of that sort of thing. I read it when I am ill and it makes me happy. I read it when I am uncomfortable and it makes me feel better. NIGEL MASDING

Outdoor Song

The more it
SNOWS – tiddely-pom
The more it
GOES – tiddely-pom
The more it
GOES – tiddely-pom
On
Snowing.

And nobody
KNOWS – tiddely-pom
How cold my
TOES – tiddely-pom
How cold my
TOES – tiddely-pom
Are
Growing.

A. A. MILNE

... because I can remember it easily and say it to myself when I'm out walking. I especially like the 'tiddely-poms', which make me laugh.

KATE DOCKING

A Cough

ahem, ahem, ahem, ahem,

I have a little cough, sir,
In my little chest, sir,
Every time I cough, sir,
It leaves a little pain, sir,
Cough,* cough, cough, cough,
There it is again, sir.

* *Or* Ahem, ahem, ahem, ahem.

ROBERT GRAVES

...because it makes me laugh. KAREN NOLAN

At the Sign of the Prancing Pony

There is an inn, a merry old inn
   beneath an old grey hill,
And there they brew a beer so brown
That the Man in the Moon himself came down
   one night to drink his fill.

The ostler has a tipsy cat
   that plays a five-stringed fiddle;
And up and down he runs his bow,
Now squeaking high, now purring low,
   now sawing in the middle.

The landlord keeps a little dog
   that is mighty fond of jokes;
When there's good cheer among the guests,
He cocks an ear at all the jests
   and laughs until he chokes.

They also keep a hornèd cow
   as proud as any queen;
But music turns her head like ale,
And makes her wave her tufted tail
   and dance upon the green.

And O! the rows of silver dishes
   and the store of silver spoons!
For Sunday there's a special pair,
And these they polish up with care
   on Saturday afternoons.

The Man in the Moon was drinking deep,
   and the cat began to wail;
A dish and a spoon on the table danced,
The cow in the garden madly pranced,
   and the little dog chased his tail.

The Man in the Moon took another mug,
   and then rolled beneath his chair;
And there he dozed and dreamed of ale,
Till in the sky the stars were pale,
   and dawn was in the air.

Then the ostler said to his tipsy cat:
   'The white horses of the Moon,
They neigh and champ their silver bits;
But their master's been and drowned his wits,
   and the Sun'll be rising soon!'

So the cat on his fiddle played hey-diddle-diddle,
   a jig that would wake the dead.
He squeaked and sawed and quickened the tune,
While the landlord shook the Man in the Moon;
   'It's after three!' he said.

They rolled the Man slowly up the hill
   and bundled him into the Moon,
While his horses galloped up in rear,
And the cow came capering like a deer,
   and a dish ran up with the spoon.

Now quicker the fiddle went deedle-dum-diddle;
   the dog began to roar,
The cow and the horses stood on their heads;
The guests all bounded from their beds
   and danced upon the floor.

With a ping and a pong the fiddle-strings broke!
   the cow jumped over the Moon,
And the little dog laughed to see such fun,
And the Saturday dish went off at a run
   with the silver Sunday spoon.

The round Moon rolled behind the hill,
   as the Sun raised up her head.
She hardly believed her fiery eyes;
For though it was day, to her surprise
   they all went back to bed!

J. R. R. TOLKIEN

... because it is jolly. DONALD NAYLOR

Upside Down

It's funny how beetles
and creatures like that
can walk upside down
as well as walk flat:

They crawl on a ceiling
and climb on a wall
without any practice
or trouble at all,

While I have been trying
for a year (maybe more)
and still I can't stand
with my head on the floor.

AILEEN FISHER

*. . . because it's rather true because I just can't stand with my head on the
floor, but I haven't been trying for one year. And it is joyable and a bit
funny.* CATHERINE FARROR

Daddy Fell into the Pond

Everyone grumbled. The sky was grey.
We had nothing to do and nothing to say.
We were nearing the end of a dismal day.
And there seemed to be nothing beyond,
   Then
      Daddy fell into the pond!

And everyone's face grew merry and bright,
And Timothy danced for sheer delight.
'Give me the camera, quick, oh quick!
He's crawling out of the duckweed!' Click!

Then the gardener suddenly slapped his knee,
And doubled up, shaking silently,
And the ducks all quacked as if they were daft,
And it sounded as if the old drake laughed.
Oh, there wasn't a thing that didn't respond
   When
      Daddy fell into the pond!

ALFRED NOYES

   … because it would be funny if my dad fell in a pond.
   ALISON BATEMAN

year olds

Upon the Snail

She goes but softly, but she goeth sure;
  She stumbles not as stronger creatures do:
Her journey's shorter, so she may endure
  Better than they which do much further go.

She makes no noise, but stilly seizeth on
  The flower or herb appointed for her food,
The which she quietly doth feed upon,
  While others range, and gare,* but find no good.

And though she doth but very softly go,
  However 'tis not fast, nor slow, but sure;
And certainly they that do travel so,
  The prize they do aim at, they do procure.

* Gare: stare about.

JOHN BUNYAN

*... because it's about a snail it describes that it goes very slow but it makes
no noise.* CLAIRE TIZARD

It was Long Ago

I'll tell you, shall I, something I remember?
Something that still means a great deal to me.
It was long ago.

A dusty road in summer I remember,
A mountain, and an old house, and a tree
That stood, you know,

Behind the house. An old woman I remember
In a red shawl with a grey cat on her knee
Humming under a tree.

She seemed the oldest thing I can remember,
But then perhaps I was not more than three.
It was long ago.

I dragged on the dusty road, and I remember
How the old woman looked over the fence at me
And seemed to know

How it felt to be three, and called out, I remember
'Do you like bilberries and cream for tea?'
I went under the tree

And while she hummed, and the cat purred, I remember
How she filled a saucer with berries and cream for me
So long ago,

Such berries and such cream as I remember
I never had seen before, and never see
Today, you know.

And that is almost all I can remember,
The house, the mountain, the grey cat on her knee,
Her red shawl, and the tree,

And the taste of the berries, the feel of the sun I remember,
And the smell of everything that used to be
So long ago,

Till the heat on the road outside again I remember,
And how the long dusty road seemed to have for me
No end, you know.

That is the farthest thing I can remember.
It won't mean much to you. It does to me.
Then I grew up, you see.

ELEANOR FARJEON

... because when I think of summer I feel nice and warm.
GARETH NEGUS

Cats

Cats sleep
Anywhere,
Any table,
Any chair,
Top of piano,
Window-ledge,
In the middle,
On the edge,
Open drawer,
Empty shoe,
Anybody's
Lap will do,
Fitted in a
Cardboard box,
In the cupboard
With your frocks –
Anywhere!
They don't care!
Cats sleep
Anywhere.

ELEANOR FARJEON

... because I have a cat and it is just like it says in the poem and I am very fond of cats. ALETTA SEYMOUR

Mice

I think mice
Are rather nice.

Their tails are long,
Their faces small,
They haven't any
Chins at all.
Their ears are pink,
Their teeth are white,
They run about
The house at night.
They nibble things
They shouldn't touch
And no one seems
To like them much.

But I think mice
Are nice.

ROSE FYLEMAN

... because I like mice. SANDRA SMITH

The Frog

Be kind and tender to the Frog,
    And do not call him names,
As 'Slimy skin', or 'Polly-wog',
    Or likewise 'Ugly James',
Or 'Gap-a-grin', or 'Toad-gone-wrong',
    Or 'Billy Bandy-knees':
The Frog is justly sensitive
    To epithets like these.
No animal will more repay
    A treatment kind and fair;
At least so lonely people say
Who keep a frog (and, by the way,
They are extremely rare).

HILAIRE BELLOC

... because there are a lot of funny words in it. And I think about it when I am sad then it makes me happy. I like to read it at bedtime and it makes me laugh. SUZANNE ELSMORE

Weather

Dot a dot dot dot a dot dot
Spotting the windowpane.

Spack a spack speck flick a flack fleck
Freckling the windowpane.

A spatter a scatter a wet cat a clatter
A splatter a rumble outside.

Umbrella umbrella umbrella umbrella
Bumbershoot barrell of rain.

Slosh a galosh slosh a galosh
Slither and slather a glide

A puddle a jump a puddle a jump
A puddle a jump puddle splosh

A juddle a pump a luddle a dump
A pudmuddle jump in and slide!

EVE MERRIAM

*. . . because of the funny words and funny rhymes. It is fun to read out loud.
I like it because I like puddles.* AMY HUTCHINS

The Caterpillar

Brown and furry
Caterpillar in a hurry,
Take your walk
To the shady leaf, or stalk,
  Or what not,
Which may be the chosen spot.
  No toad spy you,
Hovering bird of prey pass by you;
Spin and die,
To live again as butterfly.

CHRISTINA ROSSETTI

... because it is so short, simple and fun to read. I can just imagine a little fluffy 'thing' *climbing up a tree!* KYLA MCFARLANE

From a Railway Carriage

Faster than fairies, faster than witches,
Bridges and houses, hedges and ditches;
And charging along like troops in a battle,
All through the meadows the horses and cattle:
All of the sights of the hill and the plain
Fly as thick as driving rain;
And ever again, in the wink of an eye,
Painted stations whistle by.

Here is a child who clambers and scrambles,
All by himself and gathering brambles;
Here is a tramp who stands and gazes;
And there is the green for stringing the daisies!

Here is a cart run away in the road
Lumping along with man and load;
And here is a mill and there is a river:
Each a glimpse and gone for ever!

ROBERT LOUIS STEVENSON

... because it has a fast rhythm, just like a train, and I can imagine sitting on the train looking out of the window. JOSEPHINE WEISMAN

Pippa's Song

The year's at the spring,
And day's at the morn;
Morning's at seven;
The hill-side's dew-pearled;
The lark's on the wing;
The snail's on the thorn:
God's in his heaven –
All's right with the world!

ROBERT BROWNING
(from the verse drama *Pippa Passes*)

... because it sounds light and sweet. CERIS NOLAN

My Name Is ...

My name is Sluggery-wuggery
My name is Worms-for-tea
My name is Swallow-the-table-leg
My name is Drink-the-Sea.

My name is I-eat-saucepans
My name is I-like-snails
My name is Grand-piano-George
My name is I-ride-whales.

My name is Jump-the-chimney
My name is Bite-my-knee
My name is Jiggery-pokery
And Riddle-me-ree, and ME.

PAULINE CLARKE

... because it's funny and I like the names.
CATHERINE BRIDGER

The Mystery

He came and took me by the hand
    Up to a red rose tree,
He kept His meaning to Himself
    But gave a rose to me.
I did not pray Him to lay bare
    The mystery to me,
Enough the rose was Heaven to smell,
    And His own face to see.

RALPH HODGSON

... because it's like a really mysterious mystery when you read it. My best bit is when the man takes me by the hand and gives a rose to me. But I don't ask him to explain the mystery to me. That's when it's really mysterious because if you read it before you go to bed it frightens you and gives you the shivers. DOMINIC EDGINTON

Lone Dog

I'm a lean dog, a keen dog, a wild dog and lone,
I'm a rough dog, a tough dog, hunting on my own!
I'm a bad dog, a mad dog, teasing silly sheep;
I love to sit and bay the moon and keep fat souls from sleep.

I'll never be a lap dog, licking dirty feet,
A sleek dog, a meek dog, cringing for my meat.
Not for me the fireside, the well–filled plate,
But shut door and sharp stone and cuff and kick and hate.

Not for me the other dogs, running by my side,
Some have run a short while, but none of them would bide.
O mine is still the lone trail, the hard trail, the best,
Wide wind and wild stars and the hunger of the quest.

IRENE MCLEOD

... because it reminds me of when I was little I was rough and tough. It is also about an animal and I like animals. I like the bit where it says hunting on my own, because I go hunting. BRIAN FULTON

35

Blue-Butterfly Day

It is blue-butterfly day here in spring,
And with these sky-flakes down in flurry on flurry
There is more unmixed colour on the wing
Than flowers will show for days unless they hurry.

But these are flowers that fly and all but sing:
And now from having ridden out desire
They lie closed over in the wind and cling
Where wheels have freshly sliced the April mire.

ROBERT FROST

*... because it is spring now and even if it is winter it makes me feel like
spring is here. Butterflies are one of my favourite insects and when I read
this poem it makes me feel relaxed and happy.* FIONA LINDSAY

The Months

January cold desolate;
February all dripping wet;
March wind ranges;
April changes;
Birds sing in tune
  To flowers of May,
And sunny June
  Brings longest day;
In scorched July
The storm-clouds fly
Lightning-torn
August bears corn.
September fruit;
In rough October
Earth must disrobe her;
Stars fall and shoot
In keen November;
And night is long
And cold is strong
In bleak December.

CHRISTINA ROSSETTI

*... because I like long poems. I like reading them out loud because they
sound nice.* SUSAN MOLATCHIE

Vitai Lampada

There's a breathless hush in the Close tonight –
    Ten to make and the match to win –
A bumping pitch and a blinding light,
    An hour to play and the last man in.
And it's not for the sake of a ribboned coat,
    Or the selfish hope of a season's fame,
But his Captain's hand on his shoulder smote –
    'Play up! play up! and play the game!'

Extract from a poem by
SIR HENRY NEWBOLT

... because I like cricket and it sounds an exciting finish.
MICHAEL JENSEN

9 year olds

Chip the Glasses and Crack the Plates

Chip the glasses and crack the plates!
  Blunt the knives and bend the forks!
That's what Bilbo Baggins hates –
  Smash the bottles and burn the corks.

Cut the cloth and tread on the fat!
  Pour the milk on the pantry floor!
Leave the bones on the bedroom mat!
  Splash the wine on every door!

Dump the crocks in a boiling bowl;
  Pound them with a thumping pole;
And when you've finished, if any are whole,
  Send them down the hall to roll.

That's what Bilbo Baggins hates!
So, carefully! carefully with the plates!

J. R. R. TOLKIEN

... because it's funny and because it tells you what happens when you let mischievous children carry the empty plates. IAN TAYLOR

Cargoes

Quinquireme of Nineveh from distant Ophir
Rowing home to haven in sunny Palestine,
With a cargo of ivory,
And apes and peacocks,
Sandalwood, cedarwood, and sweet white wine.

Stately Spanish galleon coming from the Isthmus,
Dipping through the Tropics by the palm-green shores,
With a cargo of diamonds,
Emeralds, amethysts,
Topazes, and cinnamon, and gold moidores.

Dirty British coaster with a salt-caked smoke stack
Butting through the Channel in the mad March days,
With a cargo of Tyne coal,
Road-rail, pig-lead,
Firewood, iron-ware and cheap tin trays.

JOHN MASEFIELD

... because it gives me pictures in my mind. KATHARINE OGILVIE

The Charge of the Light Brigade

Half a league, half a league,
  Half a league onward,
All in the valley of Death
  Rode the six hundred.
'Forward the Light Brigade!
Charge for the guns!' he said:
Into the valley of Death
  Rode the six hundred.

'Forward the Light Brigade!'
Was there a man dismayed?
Not though the soldier knew
  Someone had blundered:
Theirs not to make reply,
Theirs not to reason why,
Theirs but to do and die:
Into the valley of Death
  Rode the six hundred.

Cannon to right of them,
Cannon to left of them,
Cannon in front of them
  Volleyed and thundered;
Stormed at with shot and shell,
Boldly they rode and well,
Into the jaws of Death
Into the mouth of Hell
  Rode the six hundred.

Flashed all their sabres bare,
Flashed as they turned in air,
Sabring the gunners there,

Charging an army, while
    All the world wondered:
Plunged in the battery-smoke
Right through the line they broke;
Cossack and Russian
Reeled from the sabre-stroke
    Shattered and sundered.
Then they rode back, but not,
    Not the six hundred.

Cannon to right of them,
Cannon to left of them,
Cannon behind them
    Volleyed and thundered;
Stormed at with shot and shell,
While horse and hero fell,
They that had fought so well
Came through the jaws of Death,
Back from the mouth of Hell,
All that was left of them,
    Left of six hundred.

When can their glory fade?
O the wild charge they made!
    All the world wondered.
Honour the charge they made!
Honour the Light Brigade,
    Noble six hundred!

ALFRED LORD TENNYSON

... because it gives me a wonderful, brave feeling. ELIZABETH KUTI

Macavity: the Mystery Cat

Macavity's a Mystery Cat: he's called the Hidden Paw –
For he's the master criminal who can defy the Law.
He's the bafflement of Scotland Yard, the Flying Squad's
  despair:
For when they reach the scene of crime – *Macavity's not
  there!*

Macavity, Macavity, there's no one like Macavity,
He's broken every human law, he breaks the law of gravity.
His powers of levitation would make a fakir stare,
And when you reach the scene of crime – *Macavity's not
  there!*
You may seek him in the basement, you may look up in
  the air –
But I tell you once and once again, *Macavity's not there!*

Macavity's a ginger cat, he's very tall and thin;
You would know him if you saw him, for his eyes are sunken
  in.
His brow is deeply lined with thought, his head is highly
  domed;
His coat is dusty from neglect, his whiskers are uncombed.
He sways his head from side to side, with movements like a
  snake;
And when you think he's half asleep, he's always wide
  awake.

Macavity, Macavity, there's no one like Macavity,
For he's a fiend in feline shape, a monster of depravity.
You may meet him in a by-street, you may see him in the
  square –
But when a crime's discovered, then *Macavity's not there!*

He's outwardly respectable. (They say he cheats at cards.)
And his footprints are not found in any file of Scotland
   Yard's.
And when the larder's looted, or the jewel-case is rifled,
Or when the milk is missing, or another Peke's been stifled,
Or the greenhouse glass is broken, and the trellis past
   repair –
Ay, there's the wonder of the thing! *Macavity's not there!*

And when the Foreign Office find a Treaty's gone astray,
Or the Admiralty lose some plans and drawings by the way,
There may be a scrap of paper in the hall or on the stair –
But it's useless to investigate – *Macavity's not there!*
And when the loss has been disclosed, the Secret Service
   say:
'It must have been Macavity!' – but he's a mile away.
You'll be sure to find him resting, or a-licking of his
   thumbs,
Or engaged in doing complicated long division sums.

Macavity, Macavity, there's no one like Macavity,
There never was a Cat of such deceitfulness and suavity.
He always has an alibi, and one or two to spare:
At whatever time the deed took place – MACAVITY
   WASN'T THERE!
And they say that all the Cats whose wicked deeds are
   widely known
(I might mention Mungojerrie, I might mention
   Griddlebone)

Are nothing more than agents for the Cat who all the time
Just controls their operations: the Napoleon of Crime!

T. S. ELIOT

... because we have got a cat just like Macavity who is also a thief. I also like this poem because it treats cats like humans and not like cats.
JOHN WOLSTENHOLME

The Hippopotamus's Birthday

He has opened all his parcels
          but the largest and the last;
His hopes are at their highest
          and his heart is beating fast.
O happy Hippopotamus,
          what lovely gift is here?
He cuts the string. The world stands still.
          A pair of boots appear!

O little Hippopotamus,
          the sorrows of the small!
He dropped two tears to mingle
          with the flowing Senegal;
And the 'Thank you' that he uttered
          was the saddest ever heard
In the Senegambian jungle
          from the mouth of beast or bird.

E. V. RIEU

... because it makes me feel both happy and sad, it makes me remember the happiness of opening presents. I felt the disappointment for the little hippopotamus. I thought of the jungle and the animals and creatures that live there. Is the Senegal a swampy river full of crocodiles? Who would give the hippopotamus presents and what would he get? Sometimes I wonder if the hippopotamus wore his boots and which feet he wore them on.

MARY ARMSTRONG

Where Go the Boats?

Dark brown is the river,
   Golden is the sand.
It flows along for ever,
   With trees on either hand.

Green leaves a-floating,
   Castles of the foam,
Boats of mine a-boating –
   Where will all come home?

On goes the river
   And out past the mill,
Away down the valley,
   Away down the hill.

Away down the river,
   A hundred miles or more,
Other little children
   Shall bring my boats ashore.

ROBERT LOUIS STEVENSON

*... because it is a gentle poem, and when you read it it makes you feel
happy. Also in your mind you can see the dark brown river flowing past.*
                                                    BRIDGET HOLLIGAN

Come Unto these Yellow Sands

Come unto these yellow sands,
    And then take hands:
Curtsied when you have, and kissed, –
    The wild waves whist –
Foot it featly here and there;
And, sweet sprites, the burthen bear.

Hark, hark! Bow, wow.
The watch-dogs bark: Bow, wow.
Hark, hark! I hear
The strain of strutting Chanticleer
Cry cock-a-diddle-do.

WILLIAM SHAKESPEARE
(from *The Tempest*)

... because it reminds me of the sea at night. It is a lovely poem about the sea. The waves splashing on the sand, the cry of the chanticleer. I like to think of fairies rushing over the sea, dancing and skipping over the waves.
LUCY AVERY

Jabberwocky

'Twas brillig, and the slithy toves
    Did gyre and gimble in the wabe;
All mimsy were the borogoves,
    And the mome raths outgrabe.

'Beware the Jabberwock, my son!
    The jaws that bite, the claws that catch!
Beware the Jubjub bird, and shun
    The frumious Bandersnatch!'

He took his vorpal sword in hand:
    Long time the manxome foe he sought –
So rested he by the Tumtum tree,
    And stood awhile in thought.

And as in uffish thought he stood,
    The Jabberwock, with eyes of flame,
Came whiffling through the tulgey wood,
    And burbled as it came!

One, two! One, two! And through and through
    The vorpal blade went snicker-snack!
He left it dead, and with its head
    He went galumphing back.

'And hast thou slain the Jabberwock?
   Come to my arms, my beamish boy!
O frabjous day! Callooh! Callay!'
   He chortled in his joy.

'Twas brillig, and the slithy toves
   Did gyre and gimble in the wabe;
All mimsy were the borogoves,
   And the mome raths outgrabe.

LEWIS CARROL

*... because it has so many made-up words. These words are weird words
but one can always make out what they mean – words like 'slithy' which I
think means 'slimy'. I also like it for its characters. Best of all I like the
sound of the 'frumious Bandersnatch'. My favourite verse is the fifth
verse.* JOHN HIELD

Night Mail

I

This is the night mail crossing the border,
Bringing the cheque and the postal order,

Letters for the rich, letters for the poor,
The Shop at the corner and the girl next door.

Pulling up Beattock, a steady climb –
The gradient's against her, but she's on time.

Past cotton grass and moorland boulder
Shovelling white steam over her shoulder,

Snorting noisily as she passes
Silent miles of wind-bent grasses.

Birds turn their heads as she approaches,
Stare from the bushes at her black-faced coaches.

Sheep-dogs cannot turn her course,
They slumber on with paws across.

In the farm she passes no one wakes,
But a jug in the bedroom gently shakes.

II

Dawn freshens, the climb is done.
Down towards Glasgow she descends
Towards the steam tugs yelping down the glade of cranes,
Towards the fields of apparatus, the furnaces

Set on the dark plain like gigantic chessmen,
All Scotland waits for her:
In the dark glens, beside the pale-green lochs
Men long for news.

III

Letters of thanks, letters from banks,
Letters of joy from girl and boy,
Receipted bills and invitations
To inspect new stock or visit relations,
And applications for situations
And timid lovers' declarations
And gossip, gossip from all the nations,
News circumstantial, news financial,
Letters with holiday snaps to enlarge in,
Letters with faces scrawled in the margin,
Letters from uncles, cousins, and aunts,
Letters to Scotland from the South of Fance,
Letters of condolence to Highlands and Lowlands,
Notes from overseas to Hebrides –

Written on paper of every hue,
The pink, the violet, the white and the blue,
The chatty, the catty, the boring, adoring,
The cold and official and the heart outpouring,
Clever, stupid, short and long,
The typed and printed and the spelt all wrong,

IV

Thousands are still asleep
Dreaming of terrifying monsters,
Or of friendly tea beside the band at Cranston's or
   Crawford's,

Asleep in working Glasgow, asleep in well-set Edinburgh,
Asleep in granite Aberdeen,
They continue their dreams;
And shall wake soon and long for letters,
And none will hear the postman's knock
Without a quickening of the heart,
For who can bear to feel himself forgotten?

W. H. AUDEN
(Written as a commentary for a G.P.O. film)

... because it has a nice rhythm, it is easy to remember and it has some good rhymes. In some places it is also quite funny. I like 'faces scrawled in the margin' and 'the spelt all wrong'. BEN LEAPMAN

Harrow-on-the-Hill

When melancholy Autumn comes to Wembley
    And electric trains are lighted after tea
The poplars near the Stadium are trembly
    With their tap and tap and whispering to me,
        Like the sound of little breakers
        Spreading out along the surf-line
When the estuary's filling
        With the sea.

Then Harrow-on-the-Hill's a rocky island
   And Harrow churchyard full of sailors' graves
And the constant click and kissing of the trolley buses hissing
   Is the level to the Wealdstone turned to waves
     And the rumble of the railway
     Is the thunder of the rollers
As they gather up for plunging
     Into caves.

There's a storm cloud to the westward over Kenton,
   There's a line of harbour lights at Perivale,
Is it rounding rough Pentire in a flood of sunset fire
   The little fleet of trawlers under sail?
     Can those boats be only roof tops
     As they stream along the skyline
In a race for port and Padstow
     With the gale?

JOHN BETJEMAN

*... because when you go for walks on Harrow's Hill it makes you think
of St Mary's churchyard as being full of sailors' graves, and when you
stand on the hill and see the street lights glowing they look like harbour
lights. The poem gives you a safe homecoming feeling; the harbour lights
are on, it is the end of the day and the end of the journey. I could read
the poem over and over again because it brings out my enjoyment of
familiar names and places, but it's not just that, I like the rhythm of it
and the pictures it makes in my mind.* CHRISTOPHER FRANCIS

The Snitterjipe

In mellow orchards, rich and ripe,
Is found the luminous Snitterjipe.
Bad boys who climb the bulging trees
Feel his sharp breath about their knees;
His trembling whiskers tickle so,
They squeak and squeak till they let go.
They hear his far-from-friendly bark;
They see his eyeballs in the dark
Shining and shifting in their sockets
As round and big as pears in pockets.
They feel his hot and wrinkly hide;
They see his nostrils flaming wide,
His tapering teeth, his jutting jaws,
His tongue, his tail, his twenty claws.
His hairy shadow in the moon,
It makes them sweat, it makes them swoon;
And as they climb the orchard wall
They let their pilfered pippins fall.
The Snitterjipe suspends pursuit
And falls upon the fallen fruit;
And while they flee the monster fierce,
Apples, not boys, his talons pierce.
With thumping hearts they hear him munch –
Six apples at a time he'll crunch.
At length he falls asleep, and they
On tiptoe take their homeward way.
But long before the blackbirds pipe
To welcome day, the Snitterjipe

Has fled afar, and on the green
Only his fearsome prints are seen.

JAMES REEVES

*... because as you go through the poem it gets more and more frightening
if you put real expression into it and when I heard the other class say it I
really liked it.* SOPHIE GILLIAT

Winter Morning

Winter is the king of showmen,
Turning tree stumps into snow men
And houses into birthday cakes
And spreading sugar over the lakes.
Smooth and clean and frost white
The world looks good enough to bite.
That's the season to be young,
Catching snowflakes on your tongue.

Snow is snowy when it's snowing
I'm sorry it's slushy when it's going.

OGDEN NASH

... because it sounds real. And I like the snow. SARAH JONES

The Centipede's Song

'I've eaten many strange and scrumptious dishes in my
   time,
Like jellied gnats and dandyprats and earwigs cooked in
   slime,
And mice with rice – they're really nice
When roasted in their prime.
(But don't forget to sprinkle them with just a pinch of
   grime.)

'I've eaten fresh mudburgers by the greatest cooks there
   are,
And scrambled dregs and stinkbugs' eggs and hornets
   stewed in tar,
And pails of snails and lizards' tails,
And beetles by the jar.
(A beetle is improved by just a splash of vinegar.)

'I often eat boiled slobbages. They're grand when served
   beside
Minced doodlebugs and curried slugs. And have you ever
   tried
Mosquitoes' toes and wampfish roes
Most delicately fried?
(The only trouble is they disagree with my inside.)

'I'm mad for crispy wasp-stings on a piece of buttered
   toast,
And pickled spines of porcupines. And then a gorgeous
   roast
Of dragon's flesh, well hung, not fresh –

It costs a pound at most,
(And comes to you in barrels if you order it by post.)

'I crave the tasty tentacles of octopi for tea
I like hot-dogs, I LOVE hot-frogs, and surely you'll agree
A plate of soil with engine oil's
A super recipe.
(I hardly need to mention that it's practically free.)

'For dinner on my birthday shall I tell you what I chose:
Hot noodles made from poodles on a slice of garden
    hose –
And a rather smelly jelly
Made of armadillo's toes.
(The jelly is delicious, but you have to hold your nose.)

'Now comes,' *the Centipede declared*, 'the burden of my
    speech:
These foods are rare beyond compare – some are right out
    of reach;
But there's no doubt I'd go without
A million plates of each
For one small mite,
One tiny bite
Of this FANTASTIC PEACH!'

ROALD DAHL

... because it is funny and full of nasty things. ALISON BARNETT

Spring

For, lo, the winter is past,
The rain is over and gone;
The flowers appear on the earth;
The time of the singing of birds is come,
And the voice of the turtle
   Is heard in our land;
The fig tree putteth forth her green figs,
And the vines with the tender grape
   Give a good smell.

(from 'The Song of Solomon' in
The Old Testament of The Bible)

... because it reminds me of all the things of spring that I have missed during the winter. ELSPETH ELY

year olds

The Peace-pipe

Gitche Manito, the mighty,
The creator of the nations,
Looked upon them with compassion,
With paternal love and pity;
Looked upon their wrath and wrangling
But as quarrels among children,
But as feuds and fights of children!

Over them he stretched his right hand,
To subdue their stubborn natures,
To allay their thirst and fever,
By the shadow of his right hand;
Spake to them with voice majestic,
As the sound of far off waters
Falling into deep abysses,
Warning, chiding, spake in this wise:

'O my children! my poor children!
Listen to the words of wisdom,
Listen to the words of warning,
From the lips of the Great Spirit,
From the Master of Life who made you!
I have given you lands to hunt in,
I have given you streams to fish in,
I have given you bear and bison,
I have given you roe and reindeer,
I have given you brant and beaver,
Filled the marshes full of wild-fowl,

Filled the rivers full of fishes;
Why then are you not contented?
Why then will you hunt each other?

I am weary of your quarrels,
Weary of your wars and bloodshed,
Weary of your prayers for vengeance,
Of your wranglings and dissensions;
All your strength is in your union,
All your danger is in discord;
Therefore be at peace henceforward,
And as brothers live together.'

HENRY WADSWORTH LONGFELLOW
(from *The Song of Hiawatha*)

... because I feel I am listening to a very deep voice like the great spirit (Gitche Manito). BILL NAYLOR

Stopping by Woods on a Snowy Evening

Whose woods these are I think I know.
His house is in the village, though;
He will not see me stopping here
To watch his woods fill up with snow.

My little horse must think it queer
To stop without a farmhouse near
Between the woods and frozen lake
The darkest evening of the year.

He gives his harness bells a shake
To ask if there is some mistake.
The only other sound's the sweep
Of easy wind and downy flake.

The woods are lovely, dark, and deep,
But I have promises to keep,
And miles to go before I sleep,
And miles to go before I sleep.

ROBERT FROST

... because it has a sense of mystery. There is a strong atmosphere in it. Parts are frightening like 'the darkest evening of the year', and 'but I have promises to keep'. They both mean a lot and make you think. My favourite verse is the last, I think because I am afraid, and interested in what might happen next. I also like the way the two lines 'And miles to go before I sleep, And miles to go before I sleep' repeat each other. It gives the poem a sense of ghostliness and vastness. SUZANNE KEYS

Oh, I Wish I'd looked after me Teeth

Oh, I wish I'd looked after me teeth,
   And spotted the perils beneath,
All the toffees I chewed,
   And the sweet sticky food,
Oh, I wish I'd looked after me teeth.

I wish I'd been that much more willin'
   When I had more tooth there than fillin'
To pass up gobstoppers,
   From respect to me choppers,
And to buy something else with me shillin'.

When I think of the lollies I licked,
   And the liquorice allsorts I picked,
Sherbet dabs, big and little,
   All that hard peanut brittle,
My conscience gets horribly pricked.

My mother, she told me no end,
   'If you got a tooth, you got a friend.'
I was young then, and careless,
   My toothbrush was hairless,
I never had much time to spend.

Oh I showed them the toothpaste all right,
   I flashed it about late at night,
But up-and-down brushin'
And pokin' and fussin'
   Didn't seem worth the time – I could bite!

If I'd known I was paving the way
   To cavities, caps and decay,
The murder of fillin's
   Injections and drillin's,
I'd have thrown all me sherbet away.

So I lay in the old dentist's chair,
   And I gaze up his nose in despair,
And his drill it do whine,
   In these molars of mine.
'Two amalgum,' he'll say, 'for in there.'

How I laughed at my mother's false teeth,
   As they foamed in the waters beneath.
But now comes the reckonin'
   It's *me* they are beckonin'
Oh, I *wish* I'd looked after me teeth.

PAM AYRES

It warns children to look after their teeth or else they will be sorry when they grow up. LUCY WHITEHURST

The Blackbird

In the far corner,
close by the swings,
every morning
a blackbird sings.

His bill's so yellow,
his coat's so black,
that he makes a fellow
whistle back.

Ann, my daughter,
thinks that he
sings for us two
especially.

HUMBERT WOLFE

... because I enjoy looking at the birds in the park.
MAGDA KHAWAM

The Shark

A treacherous monster is the Shark
He never makes the least remark.

And when he sees you on the sand,
He doesn't seem to want to land.

He watches you take off your clothes,
And not the least excitement shows.

His eyes do not grow bright or roll,
He has astounding self-control.

He waits till you are quite undrest,
And seems to take no interest.

And when towards the sea you leap,
He looks as if he were asleep.

But when you once get in his range,
His whole demeanour seems to change.

He throws his body right about,
And his true character comes out.

It's no use crying or appealing,
He seems to lose all decent feeling.

After this warning you will wish
To keep clear of this treacherous fish.

His back is black, his stomach white,
He has a very dangerous bite.

LORD ALFRED DOUGLAS

*... because it reminds me of when the book came through the post as a
prize. I eagerly opened it and this was the first poem I saw.*
KATHY SLATER

Pied Beauty

Glory be to God for dappled things –
   For skies of couple-colour as a brinded cow;
     For rose-moles all in stipple upon trout that swim;
Fresh-firecoal chestnut-falls; finches' wings;
   Landscape plotted and pieced – fold, fallow, and plough;
     And áll trádes, their gear and tackle and trim.

All things counter, original, spare, strange;
   Whatever is fickle, freckled (who knows how?)
     With swift, slow; sweet, sour; adazzle, dim;
He fathers-forth whose beauty is past change:
           Praise him.

GERARD MANLEY HOPKINS

... because it tells of the wonderful beauty of the world. PHILIP NOLAN

Tartary

If I were Lord of Tartary,
   Myself, and me alone,
My bed should be of ivory,
   Of beaten gold my throne;
And in my court should peacocks flaunt,
And in my forests tigers haunt,
And in my pools great fishes slant
      Their fins athwart the sun.

If I were Lord of Tartary,
   Trumpeters every day
To all my meals should summon me,
   And in my courtyards bray;
And in the evening lamps should shine,
Yellow as honey, red as wine,
While harp, and flute, and mandoline
      Made music sweet and gay.

If I were Lord of Tartary,
   I'd wear a robe of beads,
White, and gold, and green they'd be –
   And small and thick as seeds;
And ere should wane the morning star,
I'd don my robe and scimitar,
And zebras seven should draw my car
      Through Tartary's dark glades.

Lord of the fruits of Tartary,
   Her rivers silver-pale!
Lord of the hills of Tartary,
   Glen, thicket, wood, and dale!
Her flashing stars, her scented breeze,
Her trembling lakes, like foamless seas,
Her bird-delighting citron-trees,
   In every purple vale!

WALTER DE LA MARE

... because it has a good rhythm. It has lots of grandeur and splendour about it which is another reason why I like it. The idea of Tartary is lovely. ANN DEVENISH-MEARES

The Calendar

I knew when Spring was come –
Not by the murmurous hum
   Of bees in the willow-trees,
      Or frills
      Of daffodils,
   Or the scent of the breeze;
But because there were whips and tops
By the jars of lollipops
In the two little village shops.

I knew when Summer breathed –
Not by the flowers that wreathed
   The sedge by the water's edge,
      Or gold
      Of the wold,
   Or white and rose of the hedge;
But because, in a wooden box
In the window at Mrs Mock's,
There were white-winged shuttlecocks.

I knew when Autumn came –
Not by the crimson flame
   Of leaves that lapped the eaves
      Or mist
      In amethyst
   And opal-tinted weaves;
But because there were alley-taws
(Punctual as hips and haws)
On the counter at Mrs Shaw's.

I knew when Winter swirled –
Not by the whitened world,
   Or silver skeins in the lanes
      Or frost
      That embossed
  Its patterns on window-panes:
But because there were transfer-sheets
By the bottles of spice and sweets
In the shops in two little streets.

BARBARA EUPHAN TODD

*. . . because it is simple, but so beautiful. I can see and even smell the little
shops. The poem makes lovely and enchanting pictures in my imagination.
It is not long and boring and does not have complicated, impressive words
in it. It is a plain, simple but gorgeous poem, and I shall always remember
it.* HAYLEY MORGAN

Silly Old Baboon

There was a Baboon
Who, one afternoon,
Said, 'I think I will fly to the sun.'
So, with two great palms
Strapped to his arms,
He started his take-off run.

Mile after mile
He galloped in style
But never once left the ground.
'You're running too slow,'
Said a passing crow,
'Try reaching the speed of sound.'

So he put on a spurt –
By God how it hurt!
The soles of his feet caught fire.
There were great clouds of steam
As he raced through a stream
But he still didn't get any higher.

Racing on through the night,
Both his knees caught alight
And smoke billowed out from his rear.
Quick to his aid
Came a fire brigade
Who chased him for over a year.

Many moons passed by.
Did Baboon ever fly?
Did he ever get to the sun?
I've just heard today
That he's well on his way!
He'll be passing through Acton at one.

P.S. Well, what do you expect from a Baboon?

SPIKE MILLIGAN

... because it is funny but is also sad in some ways. The Baboon would probably never be able to fly anyway: it's somehow like a wild dream. I think a good rhyming part is:
'"You're running too slow,"
Said a passing crow.'

ZOË PARKER

A Song about Myself

I

There was a naughty boy,
  A naughty boy was he,
He would not stop at home,
  He could not quiet be –
    He took
    In his knapsack
    A book
    Full of vowels
    And a shirt
    With some towels –
    A slight cap
    For a night-cap –
    A hair brush,
    Comb ditto,
    New stockings,
    For old ones
    Would split O!
    This knapsack
    Tight at's back
    He rivetted close
And followed his nose
    To the North,
    To the North,
And followed his nose
To the North.

II

There was a naughty boy,
  And a naughty boy was he,

He ran away to Scotland
The people for to see –
There he found
That the ground
Was as hard,
That a yard
Was as long,
That a song
Was as merry,
That a cherry
Was as red,
That lead
Was as weighty,
That fourscore
Was as eighty,
That a door
Was as wooden
As in England –
So he stood in his shoes
And he wondered,
He wondered,
He stood in his shoes
And he wondered.

JOHN KEATS
(This is an extract from the poem)

. . . because it is long, it rhymes well and it shows that things in Scotland are the same as in England. SHARON FEELY

O Child Beside the Waterfall

O Child beside the Waterfall
What songs without a word
Rise from those waters like a call
Only a heart has heard –
The Joy, the Joy in all things
Rise whistling like a bird.

O Child beside the Waterfall
I hear them too, the brief
Heavenly notes, the harp of dawn,
The nightingale on the leaf,
All, all, dispel the darkness and
The silence of our grief.

O Child beside the Waterfall
I see you standing there,
With waterdrops and fireflies
And hummingbirds in the air,
All singing praise of paradise,
Paradise everywhere.

GEORGE BARKER

... because it is a little sad. I like poems which are sad. RACHEL HARTE

The End

When I was One,
I had just begun.

When I was Two
I was nearly new.

When I was Three
I was hardly Me.

When I was Four
I was not much more.

When I was Five
I was just alive.

But now I am Six, I'm as clever as clever.
So I think I'll be six now for ever and ever.

A. A. MILNE

*... because you cannot stay the same age and I don't know why he thinks
he is as clever as clever so he can't stay six for ever and ever. It is funny.*
PAULINE MURPHY

Extremely Naughty Children

By far
The naughtiest
Children
I know
Are Jasper
Geranium
James
And Jo.

They live
In a house
On the Hill
Of Kidd,
And what
In the world
Do you think
They did?

They asked
Their uncles
And aunts
To tea,
And shouted
In loud
Rude voices:
'We

Are tired
Of scoldings
And sendings
To bed:
Now
The grown-ups
Shall be
Punished instead.'

They said:
'Auntie Em,
You didn't
Say "Thank you!"'
They said:
'Uncle Robert,
We're going
To spank you!'

They pulled
The beard
Of Sir Henry
Dorner
And put him
To stand
In disgrace
In the corner.

They scolded
Aunt B.,
They punished
Aunt Jane;
They slapped
Aunt Louisa
Again
And again.

They said
'Naughty boy!'
To their
Uncle
Fred,
And boxed
His ears
And sent him
To bed.

Do you think
Aunts Em
And Loo
And B.,
And Sir
Henry
Dorner
(K.C.B.),

And the elderly
Uncles
And kind
Aunt Jane
Will go
To tea
With the children
Again?

ELIZABETH GODLEY

*. . . because it is funny to think of children daring to punish their relations.
Also, it was my Mum's favourite poem when she was young.*
LIESL CASTELL

The Marrog

My desk's at the back of the class
And nobody nobody knows
I'm a marrog from Mars
With a body of brass
And seventeen fingers and toes.
Wouldn't they shriek if they knew
I've three eyes at the back of my head
And my hair is bright purple
My nose is deep blue
And my teeth are half yellow half red?
My five arms are silver, and spiked with knives on them
   sharper than spears
I could go back right now if I liked –
And return in a million light years.
I could gobble them all for
I'm seven foot tall
And I'm breathing green flames from my ears.
Wouldn't they yell if they knew
If they guessed that a Marrog was here?
Ha-ha they haven't a clue –
Or wouldn't they tremble with fear!
Look, look, a Marrog
They'd all scream – and SMACK.
The blackboard would fall and the ceiling would crack
And the teacher would faint I suppose.
But I grin to myself sitting right at the back
And Nobody nobody knows.

R. C. SCRIVEN

... because I think it's funny and if I feel sad all I have to do is read this poem and I'm laughing because this poem is funny and it's not boring like some other poems I know. TRACY STANTON

11 year olds

Pleasant Sounds

The rustling of leaves under the feet in woods and under
 hedges;
The crumping of cat-ice and snow down wood-rides,
 narrow lanes, and every street causeway;
Rustling through a wood or rather rushing, while the wind
 halloos in the oak-top like thunder;
The rustle of birds' wings starled from their nests or flying
 unseen into the bushes;
The whizzing of larger birds overhead in a wood, such as
 crows, puddocks, buzzards;
The trample of robins and woodlarks on the brown leaves,
 and the patter of squirrels on the green moss;
The fall of an acorn on the ground, the pattering of nuts
 on the hazel branches as they fall from ripeness;
The flirt of the groundlark's wing from the stubbles –
 how sweet such pictures on dewy mornings, when the
 dew flashes from its brown feathers!

JOHN CLARE
(One of his late prose poems)

*... because each little picture in the poem seems to have its special sound.
I think it is a very comforting poem. This best part of the poem is at the
beginning and the last few lines. I have noticed when I have been saying
the lines out loud, there seemed a sound echoing itself later in the line.
Strange – but it could be just imagination.* PAULA MCKERRAL

Five Eyes

In Hans' old mill his three black cats
Watch his bins for the thieving rats.
Whisker and claw, they crouch in the night,
Their five eyes smouldering green and bright:
Squeaks from the flour sacks, squeaks from where
The cold wind stirs on the empty stair,
Squeaking and scampering, everywhere.
Then down they pounce, now in, now out,
At whisking tail, and sniffing snout;
While lean old Hans he snores away
Till peep of light at break of day;
Then up he climbs to his creaking mill,
Out come his cats all grey with meal –
Jekkel, and Jessup, and one-eyed Jill.

WALTER DE LA MARE

... because it isn't one of those poems that go on and on, but a not too long, not too short, very wholesome poem. I find it very interesting with just the tiniest hint of excitement. It also gives you as a kind of bonus, a sort of riddle; the first time I read it I was puzzled by the fact that there were three cats, but only five eyes for them to see with, but when I read the last line, my curiosity was completely satisfied and I wanted to read it again and again. EVA MARIE KILPATRICK

Lonely Street

I love the humble silence of this street
embellished with quiet trees
where no soul has ever gone by
except that of the wind ...
Clouds pause to look at the street
with their heavenly eyes,
and they can tell, by looking at the leaves
whether Fall or Winter have settled their realm.
I love the humble silence of this street
embellished with quiet trees
along which I walked so many Sundays
with my small grove of remembrances ...
When I die, my friend, the best of me
will survive in this street:
the concealed rose of my regrets
and the roaming music of my dreams ...

FRANCISCO LOPEZ MERINO

*... because it reminds me of my own house's street. I like the descriptions
that Francisco Lopez Merino uses and especially the last three lines.*
SYLVIA VILLALBE

Cowboy Song

I come from Salem County
  Where the silver melons grow,
Where the wheat is sweet as an angel's feet
  And the zithering zephyrs blow.
I walk the blue bone-orchard
  In the apple-blossom snow,
When the teasy bees take their honeyed ease
  And the marmalade moon hangs low.

My Maw sleeps prone on the prairie
  In a boulder eiderdown,
Where the pickled stars in their little jam-jars
  Hang in a hoop to town.
I haven't seen Paw since a Sunday
  In eighteen seventy-three
When he packed his snap in a bitty mess-trap
  And said he'd be home by tea.

Fled is my fancy sister
  All weeping like the willow.
And dead is the brother I loved like no other
  Who once did share my pillow.
I fly the florid water
  Where run the seven geese round,
O the townsfolk talk to see me walk
  Six inches off the ground.

Across the map of midnight
     I trawl the turning sky,
In my green glass the salt fleets pass,
     The moon her fire-float by.
The girls go gay in the valley
     When the boys come down from the farm,
Don't run, my joy, from a poor cowboy,
     I won't do you no harm.

The bread of my twentieth birthday
     I buttered with the sun,
Though I sharpen my eyes with lovers' lies
     I'll never see twenty-one.
Light is my shirt with lilies,
     And lined with lead my hood,
On my face as I pass is a plate of brass,
     And my suit is made of wood.

CHARLES CAUSLEY

... because this poem is full of beautiful phrases with not only lovely compositions of words but hidden meanings. 'Blue bone-orchard' is really a graveyard, and 'My Maw sleeps ... in a boulder eiderdown' means that his mother is buried beneath a boulder on the prairie.

A swinging rhythm runs through the poem. I love the line in the first verse 'Where the wheat is sweet as an angel's feet' because the very idea, apart from anything else, is such a lovely one. The last line in the eighth verse, 'I won't do you no harm', is so sad. I feel so sorry for this poor ghost of a twenty-year-old cowboy. CATHERINE PAVER

The Kingfisher

It was the Rainbow gave thee birth,
    And left thee all her lovely hues;
And, as her mother's name was Tears,
    So runs it in thy blood to choose
For haunts the lonely pools, and keep
In company with trees that weep.

Go you and, with such glorious hues,
    Live with proud Peacocks in green parks;
On lawns as smooth as shining glass,
    Let every feather show its marks;
Get thee on boughs and clap thy wings
Before the windows of proud kings.

Nay, lovely Bird, thou art not vain;
    Thou hast no proud, ambitious mind;
I also love a quiet place
    That's green, away from all mankind;
A lonely pool, and let a tree
Sigh with her bosom over me.

W. H. DAVIES

... because kingfishers are lovely birds and they go places where I like to go. LISA HINTON

The Puddock

A Puddock sat by the lochan's brim,
An' he thocht there was never a puddock like him.
He sat on his hurdies, he waggled his legs,
An' cockit his heid as he glowered throu' the seggs.*
The bigsy wee cratur' was feeling that prood,
He gapit his mou' an' he croakit oot lood:
'Gin ye'd a' like tae see a richt puddock,' quo' he,
'Ye'll never, I'll sweer, get a better nor me.
I've fem'lies an' wives an' a weel-plenished hame,
Wi' drink for my thrapple an' meat for my wame.
The lasses aye thocht me a fine strappin' chiel,
An' I ken I'm a rale bonny singer as weel.
I'm nae gaun tae blaw, but th' truth I maun tell –
I believe I'm the verra MacPuddock himsel'.'

A heron was hùngry an' needin' tae sup,
Sae he nabbit th' puddock and gollup't him up;
Syne runkled his feathers: 'A peer thing,' quo' he,
'But – puddocks is nae fat they eesed tae be.'

* Seggs: sedges.

J. M. CAIE

We had to learn this broad Scots poem for school. At first I didn't under-
stand a word of it but once it was explained to me I really began to enjoy
it. Although there is a moral to it I like the sound of the words. Puddock
really sounds better than frog, I think. KATE FORSYTH

The Way Through the Woods

They shut the road through the woods
Seventy years ago.
Weather and rain have undone it again,
And now you would never know
There was once a road through the woods
Before they planted the trees.
It is underneath the coppice and heath,
And the thin anemones.
Only the keeper sees
That, where the ring-dove broods,
And the badgers roll at ease,
There was once a road through the woods.

Yet, if you enter the woods
Of a summer evening late,
When the night-air cools on the trout-ringed pools
Where the otter whistles his mate
(They fear not men in the woods,
Because they see so few),
You will hear the beat of a horse's feet,
And the swish of a skirt in the dew,
Steadily cantering through
The misty solitudes,
As though they perfectly knew
The old lost road through the woods . . .
But there is no road through the woods!

RUDYARD KIPLING

It is very beautiful and well-written and I like it very much.
SERENA CULLEN

The Christening

What shall I call
    My dear little dormouse?
His eyes are small
    But his tail is e-nor-mouse.

I sometimes call him Terrible John,
'Cos his tail goes on –
And on –
And on.
And I sometimes call him Terrible Jack,
'Cos his tail goes on to the end of his back.
And I sometimes call him Terrible James,
'Cos he says he likes me calling him names . . .
    But I think I shall call him Jim
    'Cos I *am* fond of him!

A. A. MILNE

. . . because I am very fond of mice and also because of the ending which I think is very sweet. CLAIRE ANDREWS

I've Had This Shirt

I've had this shirt
that's covered in dirt
for years and years and years.

It used to be red
but I wore it in bed
and it went grey
cos I wore it all day
for years and years and years.

The arms fell off
in the Monday wash
and you can see my vest
through the holes in the chest
for years and years and years.

As my shirt falls apart
I'll keep the bits
in a biscuit tin
on the mantelpiece
for years and years and years.

MICHAEL ROSEN

... because the rhythm stuck fast in my head and everywhere I go I say the poem. MANDY EDWARDS

The Rivals

I heard a bird at dawn
Singing sweetly on a tree,
That the dew was on the lawn,
And the wind was on the lea;
But I didn't listen to him,
For he didn't sing to me!

I didn't listen to him,
For he didn't sing to me
That the dew was on the lawn,
And the wind was on the lea!
I was singing at the time,
Just as prettily as he!

I was singing all the time,
Just as prettily as he,
About the dew upon the lawn,
And the wind upon the lea!
So I didn't listen to him,
As he sang upon the tree!

JAMES STEPHENS

. . . because often when I read poems they are about falling autumn leaves and birds singing and soppy stuff, but when I read to the second to last line of the first verse I discovered it wasn't like it seemed it would be in the beginning and made me laugh. The writer obviously also gets fed up with soppy poems. LISA BATEMAN

The ABC

T'was midnight in the schoolroom
And every desk was shut,
When suddenly from the alphabet
Was heard a loud 'Tut-tut!'

Said A to B, 'I don't like C;
His manners are a lack.
For all I ever see of C
Is a semi-circular back!'

'I disagree,' said D to B,
'I've never found C so.
From where I stand, he seems to be
An uncompleted O.'

C was vexed, 'I'm much perplexed,
You criticize my shape.
I'm made like that, to help spell Cat
And Cow and Cool and Cape.'

'He's right,' said E; said F, 'Whoopee!'
Said G, ''Ip, 'ip, 'ooray!'
'You're dropping me,' roared H to G.
'Don't do it please I pray!'

'Out of my way,' L L said to K.
'I'll make poor I look I L L.'
To stop this stunt, J stood in front,
And presto! I L L was J I L L.

'U know,' said V, 'that W
Is twice the age of me,
For as a Roman V is five
I'm half as young as he.'

X and Y yawned sleepily,
'Look at the time!' they said.
'Let's all get off to beddy byes.'
They did, then, 'Z-z-z.'

alternative last verse

X and Y yawned sleepily,
'Look at the time!' they said.
They all jumped in to beddy byes
And the last one in was Z!

SPIKE MILLIGAN

*... because it is very imaginative and can be read over and over again
without becoming boring. It also gives me a feeling that this sort of event
really happens in schools.* ANDREW CANNING

Sea Fever

I must go down to the seas again, to the lonely sea and
   the sky,
And all I ask is a tall ship and a star to steer her by,
And the wheel's kick and the wind's song and the white
   sail's shaking,
And a grey mist on the sea's face, and a grey dawn
   breaking.

I must go down to the seas again, for the call of the
   running tide
Is a wild call and a clear call that may not be denied;
And all I ask is a windy day with the white clouds flying,
And the flung spray and the blown spume, and the
   sea-gulls crying.

I must go down to the seas again, to the vagrant gypsy
   life,
To the gull's way and the whale's way where the wind's
   like a whetted knife;
And all I ask is a merry yarn from a laughing fellow-rover,
And quiet sleep and a sweet dream when the long trick's
   over.

JOHN MASEFIELD

*... because it is pathetic. I like it because it's sad and lonely. It also
rhymes nicely.* NATASHA SMÊLE

Overheard on a Saltmarsh

Nymph, nymph, what are your beads?

Green glass, goblin. Why do you stare at them?

Give them me.

        No.

Give them me. Give them me.

            No.

Then I will howl all night in the reeds,
Lie in the mud and howl for them.

Goblin, why do you love them so?

They are better than stars or water,
Better than voices of winds that sing,
Better than any man's fair daughter,
Your green glass beads on a silver ring.

Hush, I stole them out of the moon.

Give me your beads, I want them.

            No.

I will howl in a deep lagoon
For your green glass beads, I love them so.
Give them me. Give them me.

            No.

HAROLD MONRO

... because it has a kind of mystic charm about it. I always feel sorry for the Gnome who seems to feel a great love for the beads and not just to want them out of greed. LUCY MAZDON

Not Waving but Drowning

Nobody heard him, the dead man,
But still he lay moaning:
I was much further out than you thought
And not waving but drowning.

Poor chap, he always loved larking
And now he's dead
It must have been too cold for him his heart gave way,
They said.

Oh, no no no, it was too cold always
(Still the dead one lay moaning)
I was much too far out all my life
And not waving but drowning.

STEVIE SMITH

... because it is well written and it has a clear meaning. Loneliness is something which many people suffer from but either don't admit it, or do admit it and no one realizes. This is not a very happy poem, but it describes something that most of us do not understand properly unless we are actually victims. So if you know someone that always plays about, and is always playing jokes on people, try to notice them, or they could end up like the man in the poem. CHRISTALLA PHILLIPS

Sensitive, Seldom and Sad

Sensitive, Seldom and Sad are we,
As we wend our way to the sneezing sea,
With our hampers full of thistles and fronds
To plant round the edge of the dab-fish ponds;
Oh, so Sensitive, Seldom and Sad –
Oh, *so* Seldom and Sad.

In the shambling shades of the shelving shore,
We will sing us a song of the Long Before,
And light a red fire and warm our paws
For it's chilly, it is, on the Desolate shores,
For those who are Sensitive, Seldom and Sad,
For those who are Seldom and Sad.

Sensitive, Seldom and Sad we are,
As we wander along through Lands Afar,
To the sneezing sea, where the sea-weeds be,
And the dab-fish ponds that are waiting for we
Who are, Oh, so Sensitive, Seldom and Sad,
Oh, *so* Seldom and Sad.

MERVYN PEAKE

... because it reminds me of old hunchbacks crawling about the sea like little sea creatures waiting for something to happen but as the book says it's a rhyme without a reason, so that's really why I like it.
VICTORIA GODSALL

The Unending Sky

I could not sleep for thinking of the sky,
    The unending sky, with all its million suns
Which turn their planets everlastingly
    In nothing, where the fire-haired comet runs.
If I could sail that nothing, I should cross
    Silence and emptiness with dark stars passing;
Then, in the darkness, see a point of gloss
    Burn to a glow, and glare, and keep massing,
And rage into a sun with wandering planets,
    And drop behind; and then, as I proceed,
See his last light upon his last moon's granites
    Die to a dark that would be night indeed:
Night where my soul might sail a million years
In nothing, not even Death, not even tears.

JOHN MASEFIELD

... because the poet sees space just as I see it: just black eternity with millions of stars and known and unknown planets. This poem puts you in a dreamy mood and you start to wonder about space: black eternity that goes on forever and ever. I think this poem is beautiful. UZMA HAAMEED

Tarantella

Do you remember an Inn,
Miranda?
Do you remember an Inn?
And the tedding and the spreading
Of the straw for a bedding,
And the fleas that tease in the High Pyrenees,
And the wine that tasted of tar?
And the cheers and the jeers of the young muleteers
(Under the vine of the dark verandah)?
Do you remember an Inn, Miranda,
Do you remember an Inn?
And the cheers and the jeers of the young muleteers
Who hadn't got a penny,
And who weren't paying any,
And the hammer at the doors and the Din?
And the Hip! Hop! Hap!
Of the clap
Of the hands to the twirl and the swirl
Of the girl gone chancing,
Glancing,
Dancing,
Backing and advancing,
Snapping of the clapper to the spin
Out and in –
And the Ting, Tong, Tang of the Guitar!
Do you remember an Inn,
Miranda?
Do you remember an Inn?
Never more;

Miranda,
Never more.
Only the high peaks hoar:
And Aragon a torrent at the door.
No sound
In the walls of the Halls where falls
The tread
Of the feet of the dead to the ground
No sound:
But the boom
Of the far Waterfall like Doom.

HILAIRE BELLOC

... because I like to imagine that the poet wrote it especially for me! It is a very varied poem, with, dancing, singing, etc. I imagine that 'Miranda' in the poem is an old Italian fortune-teller who is looking into her glass ball and remembering her past life when she was young and she is saying to herself, 'Never again Miranda,' meaning that she will never see or go to the Inn again because she's old. I think it's rather a sad poem, actually.

MIRANDA PERCY

A Soft Day

A soft day, thank God!
A wind from the south
With a honeyed mouth;
A scent of drenching leaves,
Briar and beech and lime,
White elder-flower and thyme
And the soaking grass smells sweet,
Crushed by my two bare feet,
While the rain drips,
Drips, drips, drips from the leaves.

A soft day, thank God!
The hills wear a shroud
Of silver cloud;
The web the spider weaves
Is a glittering net;
The woodland path is wet
And the soaking earth smells sweet
Under my two bare feet,
And the rain drips,
Drips, drips, drips from the leaves.

W. M. LETTS

*... because it is sweet. Last night's rains have washed away every speck
of dust and dirt, in the poem. The two lines I like most are:*

> *'And the soaking grass smells sweet,
> Crushed by my two bare feet.'*

*I like these lines because the word 'crushed' suggests to me a fresh, crisp
movement in which the sweet wet grass is crushed (not squashed) and lots
of goodness, and sweetness, tumbles out onto the warm earth.*

SUSIE GRUNSTEIN

Ducks' Ditty

All along the backwater,
Through the rushes tall,
Ducks are a-dabbling,
Up tails all!

Ducks' tails, drakes' tails,
Yellow feet a-quiver,
Yellow bills all out of sight
Busy in the river!

Slushy green undergrowth
Where the roach swim –
Here we keep our larder,
Cool and full and dim.

Everyone for what he likes!
We like to be
Heads down, tails up,
Dabbling free!

High in the blue above
Swifts whirl and call –
We are down a-dabbling,
Up tails all!

KENNETH GRAHAME

... because I think the endings are funny and for the first time I can say it off by heart. It makes me happy. LIANNA SKELLY

A Piper

A piper in the streets today
Set up, and tuned, and started to play,
And away, away, away on the tide
Of his music we started; on every side
Doors and windows were opened wide,
And men left down their work and came,
And women with petticoats coloured like flame.
And little bare feet that were blue with cold,
Went dancing back to the age of gold,
And all the world went gay, went gay,
For half an hour in the street today.

SEUMAS O'SULLIVAN

... because it gives you a sense of freedom and happiness.
JANE HEGARTY

Colonel Fazackerley

Colonel Fazackerley Butterworth-Toast
Bought an old castle complete with a ghost,
But someone or other forgot to declare
To Colonel Fazack that the spectre was there.

On the very first evening, while waiting to dine,
The Colonel was taking a fine sherry wine,
When the ghost, with a furious flash and a flare,
Shot out of the chimney and shivered, 'Beware!'

Colonel Fazackerley put down his glass
And said, 'My dear fellow, that's really first class!
I just can't conceive how you do it at all.
I imagine you're going to a Fancy Dress Ball?'

At this, the dread ghost gave a withering cry.
Said the Colonel (his monocle firm in his eye),
'Now just how you do it I wish I could think.
Do sit down and tell me, and please have a drink.'

The ghost in his phosphorous cloak gave a roar
And floated about between ceiling and floor.
He walked through a wall and returned through a pane
And backed up the chimney and came down again.

Said the Colonel, 'With laughter I'm feeling quite weak!'
(As trickles of merriment ran down his cheek).
'My house-warming party I hope you won't spurn.
You *must* say you'll come and you'll give us a turn!'

At this, the poor spectre – quite out of his wits –
Proceeded to shake himself almost to bits.
He rattled his chains and he clattered his bones
And he filled the whole castle with mumbles and moans.

But Colonel Fazackerley, just as before,
Was simply delighted and called out, 'Encore!'
At which the ghost vanished, his efforts in vain,
And never was seen at the castle again.

'Oh dear, what a pity!' said Colonel Fazack.
'I don't know his name, so I can't call him back.'
And then with a smile that was hard to define,
Colonel Fazackerley went in to dine.

CHARLES CAUSLEY

... because this poem is very funny. JAMES BYRNE

Eldorado

Gaily bedight,
A gallant knight
In sunshine and in shadow,
Had journeyed long,
Singing a song,
In search of Eldorado.

But he grew old –
This knight so bold –
And o'er his heart a shadow
Fell, as he found
No spot of ground
That looked like Eldorado.

And as his strength
Failed him at length,
He met a pilgrim shadow:
'Shadow,' said he,
'Where can it be,
This land of Eldorado?'

'Over the mountains
Of the Moon,
Down the valley of Shadow,
Ride, boldly ride,'
The shade replied,
'If you seek for Eldorado.'

EDGAR ALLEN POE

... because it gives you a taste of the unknown, and really makes you pity the poor knight who has wasted his whole life looking for 'Eldorado'.

LISA MANDL

I, Too

I, too, sing America.

I am the darker brother.
They send me to eat in the kitchen
When company comes,
But I laugh,
And eat well,
And grow strong.

Tomorrow,
I'll sit at the table
When company comes.
Nobody'll dare
Say to me,
'Eat in the kitchen,'
Then.

Besides,
They'll see how beautiful I am
And be ashamed –

I, too, am America.

LANGSTON HUGHES

*... because it has a nice rhythmic sound which reminds me of the Negro
Spiritual songs. Each time I read it, the poem makes me so sad to think
the boy is treated in this manner and yet happy because the boy is hopeful
about his future.* AMANDA KEMP

Granny

Through every nook and every cranny
The wind blew in on poor old Granny;
Around her knees, into each ear
(And up her nose as well, I fear).

All through the night the wind grew worse,
It nearly made the vicar curse.
The top had fallen off the steeple
Just missing him (and other people).

It blew on man; it blew on beast.
It blew on nun; it blew on priest.
It blew the wig off Auntie Fanny –
But most of all, it blew on Granny!

SPIKE MILLIGAN

*... because it is funny and my Granny complains about the wind and it
is true what the poem says.* MARY SLUGGETT

A Boy's Song

Where the pools are bright and deep,
Where the grey trout lies asleep,
Up the river and over the lea –
That's the way for Billy and me.

Where the blackbird sings the latest,
Where the hawthorn blooms the sweetest,
Where the nestlings chirp and flee,
That's the way for Billy and me.

Where the mowers mow the cleanest,
Where the hay lies thick and greenest;
There to trace the homeward bee,
That's the way for Billy and me.

Where the hazel bank is steepest,
Where the shadow falls the deepest,
Where the clustering nuts fall free,
That's the way for Billy and me.

Why the boys should drive away
Little sweet maidens from their play,
Or love to banter and fight so well,
That's the thing I never could tell.

But this I know, I love to play,
Through the meadow, among the hay;
Up the water and over the lea,
That's the way for Billy and me.

JAMES HOGG

This poem was my Grandfather's favourite poem and it describes how I like to play. SANDY BROWN

December

A wrinkled crabbèd man they picture thee,
Old Winter, with a rugged beard as grey
As the long moss upon the apple-tree;
Blue-lipt, an ice drop at thy sharp blue nose,
Close muffled up, and on thy dreary way
Plodding along through sleet and drifting snows.
They should have drawn thee by thy high-heap't hearth.
Old Winter! seated in thy great armed chair;
Watching the children at their Christmas mirth; –
Or circled by them as thy lips declare
Some merry jest, or tale of murder dire,
Or troubled spirit that disturbs the night;
Pausing at times to rouse the smouldering fire,
Or taste the old October brown and bright.

R. SOUTHEY

... because Winter is my favourite season – log fires, landscapes and snow.
In most poems winter is described as a harsh, cruel season but this poem
reminds us of all the good things that happen in this season. I also like the
poem because of the old-fashioned way it is written. HELEN MAY AYRE

The National Union of Children

NUC has just passed a weighty resolution:
'Unless all parents raise our rate of pay
This action will be taken by our members
(The resolution comes in force today):—

'Noses will not be blown (sniffs are in order),
Bedtime will get preposterously late,
Ice-cream and crisps will be consumed for breakfast,
Unwanted cabbage left upon the plate,

'Earholes and fingernails can't be inspected,
Overtime (known as homework) won't be worked,
Reports from school will all say "Could do better",
Putting bricks back in boxes may be shirked.'

The National Association of Parents

Of course, NAP's answer quickly was forthcoming
(It was a matter of emergency),
It issued to the Press the following statement
(Its Secretary appeared upon TV):—

'True that the so-called Saturday allowance
Hasn't kept pace with prices in the shops,
But neither have, alas, parental wages:
NUC's claim would ruin kind, hard-working Pops.

'Therefore, unless that claim is now abandoned,
Strike action for us, too, is what remains;
In planning for the which we are in process
Of issuing, to all our members, canes.'

ROY FULLER

*... because they are funny and bring me back to life after I have just
finished tidying my bedroom.* SUSAN BALL

Christmas

The bells of waiting Advent ring,
   The Tortoise stove is lit again
And lamp-oil light across the night
   Has caught the streaks of winter rain
In many a stained-glass window sheen
From Crimson Lake to Hooker's Green.

The holly in the windy hedge
   And round the Manor House the yew
Will soon be stripped to deck the ledge,
   The altar, font and arch and pew,
So that villagers can say
'The Church looks nice' on Christmas Day.

Provincial public houses blaze
   And Corporation tramcars clang,
On lighted tenements I gaze
   Where paper decorations hang,
And bunting in the red Town Hall
Says 'Merry Christmas to you all.'

And London shops on Christmas Eve
   Are strung with silver bells and flowers
As hurrying clerks the City leave
   To pigeon-haunted classic towers,
And marbled clouds go scudding by
The many-steepled London sky.

And girls in slacks remember Dad,
   And oafish louts remember Mum,
And sleepless children's hearts are glad,

And Christmas-morning bells say 'Come!'
Even to shining ones who dwell
Safe in the Dorchester Hotel.

And is it true? And is it true,
    This most tremendous tale of all,
Seen in a stained-glass window's hue,
    A Baby in an ox's stall?
The Maker of the stars and sea
Become a Child on earth for me?

And is it true? For if it is,
    No loving fingers tying strings
Around those tissued fripperies,
    The sweet and silly Christmas things,
Bath salts and inexpensive scent
And hideous tie so kindly meant,

No love that in a family dwells,
    No carolling in frosty air,
Nor all the steeple-shaking bells
    Can with this single Truth compare –
That God was Man in Palestine
And lives to-day in Bread and Wine.

JOHN BETJEMAN

So many people forget the real meaning of Christmas. No one seems to really know why, but just buy presents for nearly forgotten relatives because 'it's done at Christmas'. And all the time, no one remembers that 2,000 years ago, Jesus was born in Bethlehem – the First Christmas – and that is what we are supposed to be celebrating. CAITLIN MCCAWSLAND

Hard Frost

Frost called to water 'Halt!'
And crusted the moist snow with sparkling salt;
Brooks, their own bridges, stop,
And icicles in long stalactites drop,
And tench in water-holes
Lurk under gluey glass like fish in bowls.

In the hard-rutted lane,
At every footstep breaks a brittle pane,
And tinkling trees ice-bound,
Changed into weeping willows, sweep the ground;
Dead boughs take root in ponds
And ferns on windows shoot their ghostly fronds.

But vainly the fierce frost
Interns poor fish, ranks trees in an armed host,
Hangs daggers from house-eaves
And on the windows ferny ambush weaves;
In the long war grown warmer
The sun will strike him dead and strip his armour.

ANDREW YOUNG

In this poem there is something hidden and I like searching for hidden things in poems. You will find that there is something to do with war, e.g. 'strike him dead and strip his armour'. It could be said that it is an example of an extended metaphor of war. Also we have had so much snow and cold weather recently we should be able to see a picture in our mind of the descriptions. I hope you can find the hidden words and phrases about war.
O. CUNNINGHAM

Romance

When I was but thirteen or so
   I went into a golden land,
Chimborazo, Cotopaxi
   Took me by the hand.

My father died, my brother too,
   They passed like fleeting dreams.
I stood where Popocatapetl
   In the sunlight gleams.

I dimly heard the Master's voice
   And boys far-off at play,
Chimborazo, Cotopaxi
   Had stolen me away.

I walked in a great golden dream
   To and fro from school –
Shining Popocatapetl
   The dusty streets did rule.

I walked home with a gold dark boy
   And never a word I'd say,
Chimborazo, Cotopaxi
   Had taken my speech away:

I gazed entranced upon his face
   Fairer than any flower –
O shining Popocatapetl
   It was thy magic hour:

The houses, people, traffic seemed
    Thin fading dreams by day,
Chimborazo, Cotopaxi
    They had stolen my soul away!

WALTER JAMES TURNER

*... because it's so sincere and pathetic. Also it's so dream-like and I don't
know the meaning of two or three words which makes it all the more
secretish. It's the favourite of my favourite poems.*

SUSHANI FERNANDO

An Old Woman of the Roads

Oh, to have a little house!
To own the hearth and stool and all!
The heaped-up sods upon the fire,
The pile of turf against the wall!

To have a clock with weights and chains
And pendulum swinging up and down,
A dresser filled with shining delph,
Speckled and white and blue and brown!

I could be busy all the day
Clearing and sweeping hearth and floor.
And fixing on their shelf again
My white and blue and speckled store!

I could be quiet there at night
Beside the fire and by myself,
Sure of a bed and loath to leave
The ticking clock and shining delph!

Och! but I'm weary of mist and dark,
And roads where there's never a house nor bush,
And tired I am of bog and road,
And the crying wind and the lonesome hush!

And I am praying to God on high,
And I am praying him night and day,
For a little house, a house of my own
Out of the wind and the rain's way.

PADRAIC COLUM

... because it makes you really think how lucky you are living in a nice, warm, inviting house while some poor people like the lady in the poem are dreaming and hoping for this kind of luxury to occur. LINDSAY GOOD

A Welsh Testament

All right, I was Welsh. Does it matter?
I spoke a tongue that was passed on
To me in the place I happened to be,
A place huddled between grey walls
Of cloud for at least half the year.
My word for heaven was not yours.
The word for hell had a sharp edge
Put on it by the hand of the wind
Honing, honing with a shrill sound
Day and night. Nothing that Glyn Dŵr
Knew was armour against the rain's
Missiles. What was descent from him?

Even God had a Welsh name:
He spoke to him in the old language;
He was to have a peculiar care
For the Welsh people. History showed us
He was too big to be nailed to the wall
Of a stone chapel, yet still we crammed him
Between the boards of a black book.

Yet men sought us despite this.
My high cheek-bones, my length of skull
Drew them as to a rare portrait
By a dead master. I saw them stare
From their long cars, as I passed knee-deep
In ewes and wethers. I saw them stand
By the thorn hedges, watching me string
The far flocks on a shrill whistle.

And always there was their eyes' strong
Pressure on me: You are Welsh, they said;
Speak to us so; keep your fields free
Of the smell of petrol, the loud roar
Of hot tractors; we must have peace
And quietness.

                    Is a museum
Peace? I asked. Am I the keeper
Of the heart's relics, blowing the dust
In my own eyes? I am a man;
I never wanted the drab rôle
Life assigned me, an actor playing
To the past's audience upon a stage
Of earth and stone; the absurd label
Of birth, of race hanging askew
About my shoulders. I was in prison
Until you came; your voice was a key
Turning in the enormous lock
Of hopelessness. Did the door open
To let me out or yourselves in?

R. S. THOMAS

*... because I believe it shows us that, or rather me, people want you to do
one thing, but you want to do another. I think the whole idea behind the
poem is to point out how the English want Wales as a national park instead
of helping the hill-farmer or doing research into the land. If I read it I
always think it's a good example of 'stick up' for your country. The man
in the poem doesn't seem to care what the English think about him, but
what his neighbourhood think about him. All-in-all I think it's a good
poem and when in need of courage ought to be referred to.*

PAULA WOOLGAR

Far Over the Misty Mountains

Far over the misty mountains cold
To dungeons deep and caverns old
We must away ere break of day
To seek the pale enchanted gold.

The dwarves of yore made mighty spells,
While hammers fell like ringing bells
In places deep, where dark things sleep,
In hollow halls beneath the fells.

For ancient king and elvish lord
There many a gleaming golden hoard
They shaped and wrought, and light they caught
To hide in gems on hilt of sword.

On silver necklaces they strung
The flowering stars, on crowns they hung
The dragon-fire, in twisted wire
They meshed the light of moon and sun.

Far over the misty mountains cold
To dungeons deep and caverns old
We must away, ere break of day,
To claim our long-forgotten gold.

Goblets they carved there for themselves
And harps of gold; where no man delves
There lay they long, and many a song
Was sung unheard by men or elves.

The pines were roaring on the height,
The winds were moaning in the night.
The fire was red, it flaming spread;
The trees like torches blazed with light.

The bells were ringing in the dale
And men looked up with faces pale;
The dragon's ire more fierce than fire
Laid low their towers and houses frail.

The mountains smoked beneath the moon;
The dwarves, they heard the tramp of doom.
They fled their hall to dying fall
Beneath his feet, beneath the moon.

Far over the misty mountains grim
To dungeons deep and caverns dim
We must away, ere break of day,
To win our harps and gold from him!

J. R. R. TOLKIEN

This is the song the dwarves sing to Bilbo Baggins the hobbit. I chose it because I think it's a lovely mysterious poem, and you can actually enter into the mind's eye of each dwarf and see with them the mountains they sing of. You can also feel the mysterious, wishful urge of each dwarf as they sing the last verse about winning back their harps and gold from the dragon, Smaug. KATHARYN WATSON

The Donkey

When fishes flew and forests walked
    And figs grew upon thorn,
Some moment when the moon was blood
    Then surely I was born;

With monstrous head and sickening cry
    And ears like errant wings,
The devil's walking parody
    On all four-footed things.

The tattered outlaw of the earth,
    Of ancient crooked will;
Starve, scourge, deride me: I am dumb,
    I keep my secret still.

Fools! For I also had my hour;
    One far fierce hour and sweet:
There was a shout about my ears,
    And palms before my feet.

G. K. CHESTERTON

... because of the lovely way the donkey describes himself. It only reveals the donkey's true identity in the last verse as the donkey who carried Jesus on Palm Sunday. I think the words are beautiful. SUZANNE PEARSON

The Dolly on the Dustcart

I'm the dolly on the dustcart,
I can see you're not impressed,
I'm fixed above the driver's cab,
With wire across me chest,
The dustman see, he spotted me,
Going in the grinder,
And he fixed me on the lorry,
I dunno if that was kinder.

This used to be a lovely dress,
In pink and pretty shades,
But it's torn now, being on the cart,
And black as the ace of spades,
There's dirt all round me face,
And all across me rosy cheeks,
Well, I've had me head thrown back,
But we ain't had no rain for weeks.

I used to be a 'Mama' doll,
Tipped forward, I'd say 'Mum',
But the rain got in me squeaker,
And now I been struck dumb,
I had two lovely blue eyes,
But out in the wind and weather,
One's sunk back in me head like,
And one's gone altogether.

I'm not a soft, flesh-coloured dolly
Modern children like so much,
I'm one of those hard old dollies,
What are very cold to touch,
Modern dollies' underwear
Leaves me a bit nonplussed,
I haven't got a bra,
But then I haven't got a bust!

Yet I was happy in that dolls' house,
I was happy as a Queen,
I never knew that Tiny Tears
Was coming on the scene,
I heard of dolls with hair that grew,
And I was quite enthralled,
Until I realized *my* head
Was hard and pink ... and bald.

So I travels with the rubbish,
Out of fashion, out of style,
Out of me environment,
For mile after mile,
No longer prized ... dustbinized!
Unfeminine, untidy,
I'm the dolly on the dustcart.
There'll be no collection Friday.

PAM AYRES

... because I like funny long poems that are nice and simple.
JOANNE BINER

Elegy for Lyn James

I saw your manager fight. He was
Useful, but his brother had the class.
In shabby halls in Wales, or in tents
On slum ground, I saw your like
Go cuffed and bleeding from a few
Sharp rounds to set the mob aloud
Before the big men came, who had the class.

Even they did not all escape. Tim
Sheehan, whose young heart burst
In a dirty room above a fish shop;
Jerry O'Neill, bobbing his old age
Through a confusion of scattered
Fists all down the High Street; brisk
Billy Rose, blind; all these I saw.

And Jack McAvoy, swinging his right
From a wheelchair. Your murderers hide
Fatly behind the black lines of the
Regulations, your futile hands are closed
In a gloveless death. Down rotting lanes,
Behind the silent billiard hall, I hear
Your shuffling ghost, who never had the class.

LESLIE NORRIS

I didn't find this poem in a book, we were given it to learn in English. I like it because when I'm feeling depressed I read it and realize how lucky I am. I also read it when I'm angry so I can take out my feelings on the managers (the murderers), instead of somebody I could hurt. I also like it because of the change of tone of poem in the last verse from anginess to thoughtfulness. FIONA BOYLE

When I Heard the Learn'd Astronomer

When I heard the learn'd astronomer,
When the proofs, the figures, were ranged in columns
    before me,
When I was shown the charts and diagrams, to add, divide,
    and measure them,
When I sitting heard the astronomer where he lectured
    with much applause in the lecture-room,
How soon unaccountable I became tired and sick,
Till rising and gliding out I wander'd off by myself,
In the mystical moist night-air, and from time to time,
Look'd up in perfect silence at the stars.

WALT WHITMAN

*This poem soothes me and calms me down when I feel angry or sad. It
makes me think how lucky I am to be alive; we do not need learned men
to tell us how beautiful the world is, we can just go outside and look at
it.* ROSAMUND LAWS

To a Butterfly

I've watched you now a full half-hour,
Self-poised upon that yellow flower;
And, little Butterfly! indeed
I know not if you sleep or feed.
How motionless! – not frozen seas
More motionless! And then
What joy awaits you, when the breeze
Hath found you out among the trees,
And calls you forth again!

This plot of orchard-ground is ours;
My trees they are, my Sister's flowers.
Here rest your wings when they are weary;
Here lodge as in a sanctuary!
Come often to us, fear no wrong;
Sit near us on the bough!
We'll talk of sunshine and of song,
And summer days, when we were young;
Sweet childish days, that were as long
As twenty days are now.

WILLIAM WORDSWORTH

*I find it very vivid and beautiful, especially the last part, beginning from
'We'll talk of sunshine . . .' It is moving because it is so full of unmeasurable
happiness. I could read it over and over again, never getting tired with it.*
CHARMIAN EADIE

The Past

The debt is paid,
The verdict said,
The Furies laid,
The plague is stayed,
All fortunes made;
Turn the key and bolt the door,
Sweet is death forevermore.
Nor haughty hope, nor swart chagrin,
Nor murdering hate, can enter in.
All is now secure and fast;
Not the gods can shake the Past;
Flies-to the adamantine door
Bolted down forevermore.
None can re-enter there, –
No thief so politic,
No Satan with a royal trick
Steal in by window, chink, or hole,
To bind or unbind, add what lacked,
Insert a leaf, or forge a name,
New-face or finish what is packed,
Alter or mend eternal Fact.

R. W. EMERSON

... because everything in it is so true, e.g. lines 10 and 11:

'All is now secure and fast,
Not the gods can shake the Past,'

because you can't change what has happened in the past. You could make amends, perhaps, or think back at what happened, but you could never change what has happened. BECKY WOOD

Silver

Slowly, silently, now the moon
Walks the night in her silver shoon;
This way, and that, she peers, and sees
Silver fruit upon silver trees;
One by one the casements catch
Her beams beneath the silvery thatch;
Couched in his kennel, like a log,
With paws of silver sleeps the dog;
From their shadowy cote the white breasts peep
Of doves in a silver-feathered sleep;
A harvest mouse goes scampering by,
With silver claws, and silver eye;
And moveless fish in the water gleam,
By silver reeds in a silver stream.

WALTER DE LA MARE

This poem describes moonlight how I imagine it, all slow and silent but with just a bit of movement which is the harvest mouse. I also like the poem because it is mysterious and it makes me feel, when I look at the moon, that it is looking back at me. The last few lines of the poem make me say them quietly, and when I have finished I'm very silent like the moon (much to Mum's relief!). SHEENA CAVIE

The Wild, the Free

With flowing tail, and flying mane,
Wide nostrils never stretched by pain,
Mouths bloodless to the bit or rein,
And feet that iron never shod,
And flanks unscarred by spur or rod,
A thousand horse, the wild, the free,
Like waves that follow o'er the sea.

LORD BYRON
(from *Mazeppa*)

*I chose this poem by Lord Byron because I like horses and this poem
describes the horse in its natural beauty and splendour. It makes me think
that the horses are proud to be free and wild.* CATHERINE AINLEY

The Highwayman

PART ONE

The wind was a torrent of darkness among the gusty trees,
The moon was a ghostly galleon tossed upon cloudy seas,
The road was a ribbon of moonlight over the purple moor,
And the highwayman came riding –
     Riding – riding –
The highwayman came riding, up to the old inn-door.
He'd a French cocked-hat on his forehead, a bunch of lace
          at his chin,
A coat of the claret velvet, and breeches of brown doeskin:
They fitted with never a wrinkle; his boots were up to the
          thigh!

And he rode with a jewelled twinkle,
    His pistol butts a-twinkle,
His rapier hilt a-twinkle, under the jewelled sky.

Over the cobbles he clattered and clashed in the dark
            inn-yard,
And he tapped with his whip on the shutters, but all was
            locked and barred:
He whistled a tune to the window; and who should be
            waiting there
But the landlord's black-eyed daughter,
    Bess, the landlord's daughter,
Plaiting a dark red love-knot into her long black hair.

And dark in the dark old inn-yard a stable-wicket creaked
Where Tim, the ostler, listened; his face was white and
            peaked,
His eyes were hollows of madness, his hair like moldy hay;
But he loved the landlord's daughter,
    The landlord's red-lipped daughter:
Dumb as a dog he listened, and he heard the robber say –

'One kiss, my bonny sweetheart, I'm after a prize tonight,
But I shall be back with the yellow gold before the morning
            light.
Yet if they press me sharply, and harry me through the day,
Then look for me by moonlight,
    Watch for me by moonlight:
I'll come to thee by moonlight, though Hell should bar the way.'

He rose upright in the stirrups, he scarce could reach her
           hand;
But she loosened her hair i'the casement! His face burnt
           like a brand
As the black cascade of perfume came tumbling over his
           breast;
And he kissed its waves in the moonlight,
    (Oh, sweet black waves in the moonlight)
Then he tugged at his reins in the moonlight, and galloped
           away to the West.

PART TWO

He did not come in the dawning; he did not come at noon;
And out of the tawny sunset, before the rise o' the moon,
When the road was a gypsy's ribbon, looping the purple
           moor,
A red-coat troop came marching –
    Marching – marching –
King George's men came marching, up to the old inn-door.

They said no word to the landlord, they drank his ale
           instead;
But they gagged his daughter and bound her to the foot of
           her narrow bed.
Two of them knelt at her casement, with muskets at the
           side!
There was death at every window;
    And Hell at one dark window;
For Bess could see, through her casement, the road that
           he would ride.

They had tied her up to attention, with many a sniggering
        jest:
They had bound a musket beside her, with the barrel
        beneath her breast!
'Now keep good watch!' and they kissed her.
    She heard the dead man say –

Look for me by moonlight;
    Watch for me by moonlight;
I'll come to thee by moonlight, though Hell should bar the way!

She twisted her hands behind her; but all the knots held
        good!
She writhed her hands till her fingers were wet with sweat
        or blood!
They stretched and strained in the darkness, and the hours
        crawled by like years;
Till, now, on the stroke of midnight,
    Cold, on the stroke of midnight,
The tip of one finger touched it! The trigger at least was
        hers!

The tip of one finger touched it; she strove no more for
        the rest!
Up, she stood up to attention, with the barrel beneath her
        breast,
She would not risk their hearing: she would not strive again;
For the road lay bare in the moonlight,
    Blank and bare in the moonlight;
And the blood of her veins in the moonlight throbbed to
        her Love's refrain.

Tlot-tlot, tlot-tlot! Had they heard it? The horse-hoofs
      ringing clear –
Tlot-tlot, tlot-tlot, in the distance? Were they deaf that
      they did not hear?
Down the ribbon of moonlight, over the brow of the hill,
The highwayman came riding,
    Riding, riding!
The red-coats looked to their priming! She stood up
      straight and still!

Tlot-tlot, in the frosty silence! *Tlot-tlot* in the echoing night!
Nearer he came and nearer! Her face was like a light!
Her eyes grew wide for a moment; she drew one last deep
      breath,
Then her finger moved in the moonlight,
    Her musket shattered the moonlight,
Shattered her breast in the moonlight and warned him –
      with her death.

He turned; he spurred him westward; he did not know
      who stood
Bowed with her head o'er the musket, drenched with her
      own red blood!
Not till the dawn he heard it, and slowly blanched to hear
How Bess, the landlord's daughter,
    The landlord's black-eyed daughter,
Had watched for her Love in the moonlight; and died in
      the darkness there.

Back, he spurred like a madman, shrieking a curse to the
      sky,
With the white road smoking behind him, and his rapier
      brandished high!

Blood-red were his spurs i'the golden noon; wine-red was
       his velvet coat;
When they shot him down on the highway,
    Down like a dog on the highway,
And he lay in his blood on the highway, with the bunch of
       lace at his throat.

*

And still of a winter's night, they say, when the wind is in the
       trees,
When the moon is a ghostly galleon tossed upon cloudy seas,
When the road is a ribbon of moonlight over the purple moor,
A highwayman comes riding –
    Riding – riding –
A highwayman comes riding, up to the old inn-door.

Over the cobbles he clatters and clangs in the dark inn-yard;
And he taps with his whip on the shutters, but all is locked
      and barred:
He whistles a tune to the window, and who should be waiting
      there
But the landlord's black-eyed daughter,
    Bess, the landlord's daughter,
Plaiting a dark red love-knot into her long black hair.

ALFRED NOYES

... *because:*
1. *rhythm – the rhythm is like the beating of a horse's hooves and gives
   the poem a lovely atmosphere.*
2. *descriptions – these are very good. They give polish to the poem.*
3. *the wording – this, like the rhythm, adds atmosphere. It is written in a
   kind of bold romantic style that makes the story it is telling more vivid.*
4. *well written – the poem is written in a very sensitive way. I often cry
   after reading it. The tension is built up very well.* CEINWEN JONES

14 year olds

My Brother is Making a Protest about Bread

My brother is making a protest about bread.
'Why do we always have wholemeal bread?
You can't spread the butter on wholemeal bread,
you try to spread the butter on
and it just makes a hole right through the middle.'

He marches out of the room and shouts
across the landing and down the passage.
'It's always the same in this place.
Nothing works.
The volume knob's broken on the radio you know,
it's been broken for months and months you know.'

He stamps back into the kitchen
stares at the loaf of bread and says:
'Wholemeal bread – look at it, look at it.
You put the butter on
and it all rolls up,
you put the butter on
and it all rolls up.'

MICHAEL ROSEN

*... because I can easily identify with it. I am a long sufferer of wholemeal
bread, and have also found a tendency for the middle to roll up when butter
is applied! My family never seem to get things mended when broken, until
they have been lying around a long time, and this often irritates me. I'm
glad someone else shares my point of view!* AMANDA HOWARD

Fidele's Dirge

Fear no more the heat o' the sun,
   Nor the furious winter's rages;
Thou thy worldly task hast done,
   Home art gone, and ta'en thy wages:
Golden lads and girls all must,
As chimney-sweepers, come to dust.

Fear no more the frown o' the great,
   Thou art past the tyrant's stroke;
Care no more to clothe and eat;
   To thee the reed is as the oak:
The sceptre, learning, physic, must
All follow this, and come to dust.

Fear no more the lightning-flash,
   Nor the all-dreaded thunder-stone;
Fear not slander, censure rash;
   Thou hast finished joy and moan:
All lovers young, all lovers must,
Consign to thee, and come to dust.

WILLIAM SHAKESPEARE
(from *Cymbeline*)

. . . because it is so exhilarating. It sweeps me along in the splendid, stormy words, then there is the quiet, peaceful lagoon of the last two lines of each verse. It is a wonderful poem, as hard, proud and fierce as a rock in a storm. THERESA KANE

The Lady of Shalott

Part I

On either side the river lie
Long fields of barley and of rye,
That clothe the wold and meet the sky;
And through the field the road runs by
     To many-towered Camelot;
And up and down the people go,
Gazing where the lilies blow
Round an island there below,
     The island of Shalott.

Willows whiten, aspens quiver,
Little breezes dusk and shiver
Through the wave that runs for ever
By the island in the river
     Flowing down to Camelot.
Four grey walls, and four grey towers,
Overlook a space of flowers,
And the silent isle imbowers
     The Lady of Shalott.

By the margin, willow-veiled,
Slide the heavy barges trailed
By slow horses; and unhailed
The shallop flitteth silken-sailed
     Skimming down to Camelot;
But who hath seen her wave her hand?
Or at the casement seen her stand?
Or is she known in all the land,
     The Lady of Shalott?

Only reapers, reaping early
In among the bearded barley,
Hear a song that echoes cheerly
From the river winding clearly,
    Down to towered Camelot:
And by the moon the reaper weary,
Piling sheaves in uplands airy,
Listening, whispers, ''Tis the fairy
    Lady of Shalott.'

ALFRED LORD TENNYSON

... because it has got so much mystery and eeriness to it. It makes you feel as if you are actually there on the island of Shalott. I always imagine myself as the romantic Lady of Shalott. It is also beautifully written with lovely flowing words which glide along gracefully. SARAH BOOKER

A Boy's Head

In it there is a space-ship
and a project
for doing away with piano lessons.

And there is
Noah's ark,
which shall be first.

And there is
an entirely new bird,
an entirely new hare,
an entirely new bumble-bee.

There is a river
that flows upwards.

There is a multiplication table.

There is anti-matter.

And it just cannot be trimmed.

I believe
that only what cannot be trimmed
is a head.

There is much promise
in the circumstance
that so many people have heads.

MIROSLAV HOLUB

... because of its humour, reality and perception. I love the project for doing away with piano lessons: how vividly I remember those awful half-an-hour-once-a-week times when I'd never practised and always got a frosty eye boring into me as my hands nervously shook when playing the allotted piece! CAROLINE MCADAM

The Paint Box

'Cobalt and umber and ultramarine,
Ivory black and emerald green –
What shall I paint to give pleasure to you?'
'Paint for me somebody utterly new.'

'I have painted you tigers in crimson and white.'
'The colours were good and you painted aright.'
'I have painted the cook and a camel in blue
And a panther in purple.' 'You painted them true.

Now mix me a colour that nobody knows,
And paint me a country where nobody goes,
And put in it people a little like you,
Watching a unicorn drinking the dew.'

E. V. RIEU

... because it is very relaxing and I like to read it because I can imagine all the things painted and their colour. My favourite part is the last stanza of something utterly new that no one has ever painted before with a beautiful new colour. MICHELLE MILLINGTON-BUCK

On a Portrait of a Deaf Man

The kind old face, the egg-shaped head,
    The tie, discreetly loud,
The loosely fitting shooting clothes,
    A closely fitting shroud.

He liked Old City dining-rooms,
    Potatoes in their skin,
But now his mouth is wide to let
    The London clay come in.

He took me on long silent walks
    In country lanes when young,
He knew the name of every bird
    But not the song it sung.

And when he could not hear me speak
    He smiled and looked so wise
That now I do not like to think
    Of maggots in his eyes.

He liked the rain-washed Cornish air
    And smell of ploughed-up soil,
He liked a landscape big and bare
    And painted it in oil.

But least of all he liked that place
    Which hangs on Highgate Hill
Of soaked Carrara-covered earth
    For Londoners to fill.

He would have liked to say good-bye,
    Shake hands with many friends,
In Highgate now his finger-bones
    Stick through his finger-ends.

You, God, who treat him thus and thus,
    Say 'Save his soul and pray.'
You ask me to believe You and
    I only see decay.

JOHN BETJEMAN

... because it may seem a little grisly and morbid but I think it is very
moving. One of the reasons I am so moved by it is because I had a Grandad
who was deaf, who I loved very much, and he died tragically with no
forewarning. IAN LAND

Boy at the Window

Seeing the snowman standing all alone
In dusk and cold is more than he can bear.
The small boy weeps to hear the wind prepare
A night of gnashings and enormous moan.
His tearful sight can hardly reach to where
The pale-faced figure with bitumen eyes
Returns him such a god-forsaken stare
As outcast Adam gave to Paradise.

The man of snow is, nonetheless, content,
Having no wish to go inside and die.
Still, he is moved to see the youngster cry.
Though frozen water is his element,
He melts enough to drop from one soft eye
A trickle of the purest rain, a tear
For the child at the bright pane surrounded by
Such warmth, such light, such love, and so much fear.

RICHARD WILBUR

... because it makes me feel sad and yet happy as well, and it also makes me feel calm and thoughtful. If I am in a bad mood, this poem makes me feel happy and very relaxed. LISA WATT

Old Meg

Old Meg she was a Gipsey,
   And liv'd upon the Moors;
Her bed it was the brown heath turf,
   And her house was out of doors.

Her apples were swart blackberries,
   Her currants, pods o'broom;
Her wine was dew of the wild white rose,
   Her book a churchyard tomb.

Her Brothers were the craggy hills,
   Her Sisters larchen trees;
Alone with her great family
   She liv'd as she did please.

No breakfast had she many a morn,
   No dinner many a noon,
And, 'stead of supper, she would stare
   Full hard against the moon.

But every morn, of woodbine fresh
   She made her garlanding,
And, every night, the dark glen Yew
   She wove, and she would sing.

And with her fingers, old and brown,
   She plaited Mats o' Rushes,
And gave them to the cottagers
   She met among the Bushes.

Old Meg was brave as Margaret Queen
  And tall as Amazon;
An old red blanket cloak she wore,
  A chip hat had she on.
God rest her aged bones somewhere!
  She died full long agone!

JOHN KEATS

... because 'Meg Merrilies' seems to have an alternative to everything she does not possess. For example, she did not have a proper house so she lived out of doors and slept on brown heath turf because she did not have a bed. She had no books so she read the grave-stones in the churchyard. She had no family so she made the hills and trees her brothers and sisters.

DAWN CURWELL

Self-Pity

I never saw a wild thing
sorry for itself.
A small bird will drop frozen dead from a bough
without ever having felt sorry for itself.

D. H. LAWRENCE

When I am feeling sorry for myself, this short, sweet little poem often comes to mind and, somehow, it has a warming influence. I don't really know why ... it is quite a morbid little meaning that it portends, and not a very cheering subject. AMBREEN HAMEED

Chamber Music

Lean out of the window,
    Golden hair,
I hear you singing
    A merry air.

My book is closed;
    I read no more,
Watching the fire dance
    On the floor.

I have left my books:
    I have left my room:
For I heard you singing
    Through the gloom.

Singing and singing
    A merry air.
Lean out of the window,
    Golden hair.

JAMES JOYCE

... because it reminds me of the best fairy tales, such as Rapunzel singing from a turret window at dusk. It's only coincidence that I found the poem, from a friend's copy of the book. It is reassuringly old-fashioned and chivalrous. Altogether 'Chamber Music' is quietly inspiring and my favourite poem. CHARLOTTE WOODWARD

If —

If you can keep your head when all about you
    Are losing theirs and blaming it on you;
If you can trust yourself when all men doubt you,
    But make allowance for their doubting too;
If you can wait and not be tired by waiting,
    Or, being lied about, don't deal in lies,
Or, being hated, don't give way to hating,
    And yet don't look too good, nor talk too wise;

If you can dream – and not make dreams your master;
    If you can think – and not make thoughts your aim;
If you can meet with triumph and disaster
    And treat those two impostors just the same;
If you can bear to hear the truth you've spoken
    Twisted by knaves to make a trap for fools,
Or watch the things you gave your life to broken,
    And stoop and build 'em up with wornout tools;

If you can make one heap of all your winnings
    And risk it on one turn of pitch-and-toss,
And lose, and start again at your beginnings
    And never breathe a word about your loss;
If you can force your heart and nerve and sinew
    To serve your turn long after they are gone,
And so hold on when there is nothing in you
    Except the Will which says to them: 'Hold on';

If you can talk with crowds and keep your virtue,
  Or walk with kings – nor lose the common touch;
If neither foes nor loving friends can hurt you;
  If all men count with you, but none too much;
If you can fill the unforgiving minute
  With sixty seconds' worth of distance run –
Yours is the Earth and everything that's in it,
  And – which is more – you'll be a Man, my son!

RUDYARD KIPLING

... because it gives me a lot of encouragement and I like the way it is written. Rudyard Kipling is my favourite poet, and I also like 'The 'Eathen' and 'The Gods of the Copybook Headings' very much. I think the poem gives lots of good advice, and I have learnt it off by heart.

I had to pick three poems instead of just one, because each of these IS my favourite one, and I just couldn't choose between them. They are all something special to me, so I decided to send all three. I hope you don't mind. (Editor's note: the other two were 'Horses' by Edwin Muir, and 'This is Going to Hurt Just a Little Bit' by Ogden Nash.)

MELISSA WYPER

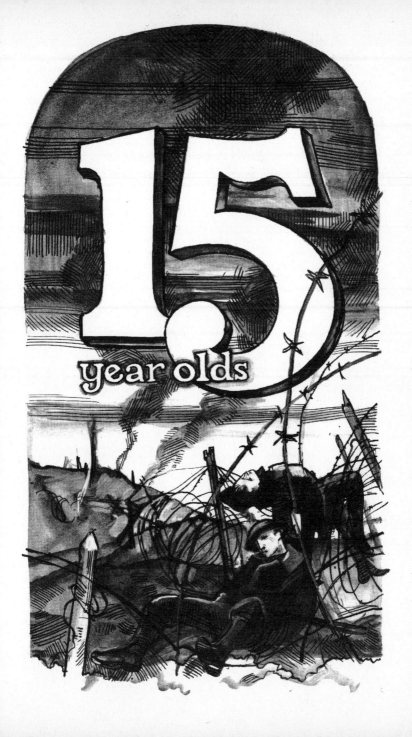

Anthem for Doomed Youth

What passing-bells for these who die as cattle?
  Only the monstrous anger of the guns.
  Only the stuttering rifles' rapid rattle
Can patter out their hasty orisons.
No mockeries for them from prayers or bells,
  Nor any voice of mourning save the choirs, –
The shrill, demented choirs of wailing shells;
  And bugles calling for them from sad shires.

What candles may be held to speed them all?
  Not in the hands of boys, but in their eyes
Shall shine the holy glimmers of good-byes.
  The pallor of girls' brows shall be their pall;
Their flowers the tenderness of silent minds,
And each slow dusk the drawing-down of blinds.

WILFRED OWEN

*. . . because of its beautiful rhythm and the way Owen has used words in it.
I love 'the stuttering rifles' rapid rattle' because all the 'r's' really do
suggest gunfire, as does 'stuttering'. I think the last line of all is the most
beautiful, to me it is the slow closing of eyes in one who is gradually dying.
The twilight world of peace.*

*This poem is so sad and so lovely, and my favourite. When I am feeling
cross with someone or ill-tempered with the world in general, I read it and
it reminds me that some have gone through hell, and perhaps my troubles
are smaller than I previously thought.* JANE WINFIELD

Memorabilia

Ah, did you once see Shelley plain,
    And did he stop and speak to you
And did you speak to him again?
    How strange it seems and new!

But you were living before that,
    And also you are living after;
And the memory I started at –
    My starting moves your laughter.

I crossed a moor, with a name of its own
    And a certain use in the world no doubt,
Yet a hand's-breadth of it shines alone
    'Mid the blank miles round about:

For there I picked up on the heather
    And there I put inside my breast
A moulted feather, an eagle-feather!
    Well, I forget the rest.

ROBERT BROWNING

... it gives me a feeling of excitement that is hard to explain and the other strange thing is that although it was written about a hundred years ago it seems quite modern. DAVID LEWIS

Adlestrop

Yes. I remember Adlestrop –
The name, because one afternoon
Of heat the express-train drew up there
Unwontedly. It was late June.

The steam hissed. Someone cleared his throat.
No one left and no one came
On the bare platform. What I saw
Was Adlestrop – only the name

And willows, willow-herb, and grass,
And meadowsweet, and haycocks dry,
No whit less still and lonely fair
Than the high cloudlets in the sky.

And for that minute a blackbird sang
Close by, and round him, mistier,
Farther and farther, all the birds
Of Oxfordshire and Gloucestershire.

EDWARD THOMAS

*I find this poem peaceful and tranquil in tone, and when reading it I
always feel soothed and calmed. I particularly like the final line as the
thought of all those birds singing at once delights and fascinates me.*

FIONA CUMBERPATCH

Clowns

Zing! goes the cymbal. Bang! goes the drum,
See how they tipple-topple-tumbling come,
Dazing the country, dazzling the towns,
Here's the procession of the circus clowns.

Hop on the heel and twist on the toe,
See how they wibble-wabble-waddling go.
Bim-bam-balloons in the clear blue air!
Clowns on the march to they-don't-know-where

Painted-on-smiles that are long and loud
Beam at the giggle-goggling crowd,
Under the paint do they grin so gay?
Nobody sees so I just can't say.

Look how the clowns all a-cantering come
Riding their donkeys with a hee-haw-hum.
Where have they come from? where do they go?
They kin-can't say for they din-don't know.

MARGARET MAHY

... because it is so gay and joyful and by reading it an image of happy dancing clowns can be seen. In each verse there are happy, funny and exciting words which make this my favourite poem. LORNA GAY

There are Four Things

There are four things that are too
mysterious for me to understand:
An eagle flying in the sky,
a snake moving on a rock,
a ship finding its way over the sea,
and a man and a woman falling in love.

GOOD NEWS BIBLE

It's the kind of poetry that when you have read it, you want to read it again – more slowly – and understand it more clearly. When I first read it, I liked it so much that I wrote it out on a sheet of paper, drew a frame of flowers around it and put it on the wall! SARA HAMMOND

To Autumn

Season of mists and mellow fruitfulness,
  Close bosom-friend of the maturing sun,
Conspiring with him how to load and bless
  With fruit the vines that round the thatch-eves run;
To bend with apples the mossed cottage-trees,
  And fill all fruit with ripeness to the core;
    To swell the gourd, and plump the hazel shells
  With a sweet kernel; to set budding more,
And still more, later flowers for the bees,
Until they think warm days will never cease,
    For Summer has o'er-brimmed their clammy cells.

Who hath not seen thee oft amid thy store?
  Sometimes whoever seeks abroad may find
Thee sitting careless on a granary floor,
  Thy hair soft-lifted by the winnowing wind;
Or on a half-reaped furrow sound asleep,
  Drowsed with the fume of poppies, while thy hook
    Spares the next swath and all its twinèd flowers;
And sometimes like a gleaner thou dost keep
  Steady thy laden head across a brook;
  Or by a cider-press, with patient look,
    Thou watchest the last oozings hours by hours.

Where are the songs of Spring? Ay, where are they?
  Think not of them, thou hast thy music too –
While barrèd clouds bloom the soft-dying day,
  And touch the stubble-plains with rosy hue:

Then in a wailful choir the small gnats mourn
   Among the river sallows, borne aloft
     Or sinking as the light wind lives or dies;
And full-grown lambs loud bleat from hilly bourn;
   Hedge-crickets sing; and now with treble soft
   The red-breast whistles from a garden-croft;
     And gathering swallows twitter in the skies.

JOHN KEATS

... it sums up all the best things about my favourite time of the year. As I read I can almost feel in my eyes the warmth of the weakening, 'maturing sun' and my mouth begins to water as I think of the honey from bees.

The poem also gives me a sense of nostalgia, as it evokes memories of growing up in the country. I remember the haze of warm, chaff-moted air, turbulent in the wake of a combine harvester. I feel a heaviness in my head when I think of the still, burdening air lining streams, as Autumn keeps 'steady thy laden head across a brook', especially in evenings, when 'in a wailful choir the small gnats mourn Among the river sallows ...' I hear my mother calling at the back of my mind, for me to come in for bedtime. PENELOPE HOWARD

The Listeners

'Is there anybody there?' said the Traveller,
    Knocking on the moonlit door;
And his horse in the silence champed the grasses
    Of the forest's ferny floor:
And a bird flew up out of the turret,
    Above the Traveller's head:
And he smote upon the door a second time;
    'Is there anybody there?' he said.
But no one descended to the Traveller;
    No head from the leaf-fringed sill
Leaned over and looked into his grey eyes,
    Where he stood perplexed and still.
But only a host of phantom listeners
    That dwelt in the lone house then
Stood listening in the quiet of the moonlight
    To that voice from the world of men:
Stood thronging the faint moonbeams on the dark stair,
    That goes down to the empty hall,
Hearkening in an air stirred and shaken
    By the lonely Traveller's call.
And he felt in his heart their strangeness,
    Their stillness answering his cry,
While his horse moved, cropping the dark turf,
    'Neath the starred and leafy sky;
For he suddenly smote on the door, even
    Louder, and lifted his head: –
'Tell them I came, and no one answered,
    That I kept my word,' he said.
Never the least stir made the listeners,
    Though every word he spake

Fell echoing through the shadowiness of the still house
    From the one man left awake:
Ay, they heard his foot upon the stirrup,
    And the sound of iron on stone,
And how the silence surged softly backward,
    When the plunging hoofs were gone.

WALTER DE LA MARE

... because it has such lovely word patterns, but also because it describes perfectly the creepy feeling when you come upon an old house in a wood that the inhabitants are still there, watching you, silently, waiting for you to be gone. ALISON SIMPSON

I hoped that, with the brave ...

I hoped that, with the brave and strong
    My portioned task might lie;
To toil amid the busy throng,
    With purpose pure and high.

ANNE BRONTË
(one verse of many from *Last Lines*)

When I read this short poem, it made me feel a lot better and cheered me up, so now, whenever I am feeling down I think of it and it comforts me. I often find myself repeating it, not always when I am feeling down. This is the only poetry I know which has been written by Anne Brontë and it is certainly my favourite poem. VANESSA FOOT

Ozymandias

I met a traveller from an antique land
Who said: Two vast and trunkless legs of stone
Stand in the desert . . . Near them, on the sand,
Half sunk, a shattered visage lies, whose frown,
And wrinkled lip, and sneer of cold command,
Tell that its sculptor well those passions read
Which yet survive, stamped on these lifeless things,
The hand that mocked them, and the heart that fed:
And on the pedestal these words appear:
'My name is Ozymandias, king of kings:

Look on my works, ye Mighty, and despair!'
Nothing beside remains. Round the decay
Of that colossal wreck, boundless and bare
The lone and level sands stretch far away.

PERCY BYSSHE SHELLEY

... because of the fantastic use of words to conjure up images of the hot desert and the fall of a proud king. The name 'Ozymandias' has a strange resonance which creates an air of mystery. HELEN PUTMAN

Under the Hazy, Blossom-laden Sky

Under the hazy, blossom-laden sky
The city sprawls, its gaping wounds exposed:
The streets due for a surgical operation,
Canals gathering pitch and filth,
Bridges with their concrete peeling away.

Under the hazy, blossom-laden sky
Cranes moving,
Drain-pipes lined up,
Truck after truck
Carrying dirt, rubbish, mud,
The burnt-out, festering hulks of war.

Dark caverns in the streets:
On the canal bed, submerged groans and sighs
Of those who will not surface:
Methane gushing up.

In the city with those clogged wounds
International streets will appear soon,
Rows of gay shops will grow,
Tempting goods will brighten the windows.

Under the hazy, blossom-laden sky
New building goes on.
Our ears tuned to the detonations under the hazy,
    blossom-laden sky,
We pray
That the fire-rain never again fall on the world.

OKAMOTO JUN

*... because it reveals to me the horror and senselessness of war — not
because that delights me but because it helps me to realize how wrong war
is and how senseless and destructive. I also like it because it shows the
determination of man to put all the evil of war behind him and restart the
life he had been living but with one difference — non-wish for war.*
KATHERINE YOUNG

Reeds of Innocence

Piping down the valleys wild,
    Piping songs of pleasant glee,
On a cloud I saw a child,
    And he laughing said to me:

'Pipe a song about a Lamb!'
    So I piped with merry cheer.
'Piper, pipe that song again';
    So I piped: he wept to hear.

'Drop thy pipe, thy happy pipe;
    Sing thy songs of happy cheer':
So I sang the same again,
    While he wept with joy to hear.

'Piper, sit thee down and write
    In a book, that all may read.'
So he vanished from my sight,
    And I plucked a hollow reed,

And I made a rural pen,
    And I stained the water clear,
And I wrote my happy songs
    Every child may joy to hear.

WILLIAM BLAKE

When I first read it, I at once thought of my childhood. I remembered how we played (i.e. my sister and brother). At that time, we were innocent children as we did not even know one problem that existed. Today, when you think of these days, it is really sad. All that we did is not to be found in a dream nowadays. BALLGOBIN REHOUTEE

Acknowledgements

The editor and publishers wish to thank the following for permission to use copyright material in this collection:

The Song of Solomon from the Authorized Version of the Holy Bible is Crown Copyright and extracts used herein are with permission.

Faber & Faber Ltd for 'Night Mail' from *Collected Poems* by W. H. Auden; Pam Ayres for 'Oh, I Wish I'd looked after me Teeth' and 'The Dolly on the Dustcart' from *All Pam's Poems* (Hutchinson); Faber & Faber Ltd for 'O Child Beside the Waterfall' from *To Alysham Fair* by George Barker; Gerald Duckworth & Co. Ltd for 'The Frog' by Hilaire Belloc from *Cautionary Verses*; A. D. Peters & Co. Ltd on behalf of the Estate of Hilaire Belloc for 'Tarantella' from *Sonnets and Verse* (Duckworth); Sir John Betjeman and John Murray (Publishers) Ltd for 'Harrow-on-the-Hill', 'Christmas' and 'On a Portrait of a Deaf Man', from *Collected Poems*; J. M. Caie for 'The Puddock' from *The Scots Kist* published by Oliver & Boyd on behalf of The Burns Federation; Charles Causley for 'Cowboy Song' from *Union Street* (Macmillan) and 'Colonel Fazackerley' from *Figgie Hobbin* (Macmillan); the Estate of the late G. K. Chesterton for 'The Donkey' from *The Collected Poems of G. K. Chesterton* (Methuen); Abelard-Schuman Ltd for 'My Name Is ...' by Pauline Clarke from *Silver Bells and Cockle Shells*; Roald Dahl and George Allen & Unwin (Publishers) Ltd for 'The Centipede's Song' from *James and the Giant Peach*; the Estate of W. H. Davies and Jonathan Cape Ltd for 'The Kingfisher' from *The Complete Poems of W. H. Davies*; The Literary Trustees of Walter de la Mare and The Society of Authors as their representative for 'Five Eyes', 'Tartary', 'Silver' and 'The Listeners'; Edward Colman, Literary Executor of Lord Alfred Douglas, for 'The Shark' from *Tales with a Twist* (Edward Arnold); Faber & Faber Ltd for 'Macavity: the Mystery Cat' from *Old Possum's Book of Practical Cats* by T. S. Eliot; Michael Joseph Ltd for 'It was Long Ago' from *Silver Sand and Snow* by Eleanor Farjeon; Oxford University Press for 'Cats' from *The Children's Bells* by Eleanor Farjeon; Aileen Fisher for 'Upside Down' from *Up the Windy Hill* (Abelard-Schuman); Jonathan Cape Ltd and the Estate of Robert Frost for 'Blue-Butterfly

Collected Poems of Ogden Nash (Dent); Peter Newbolt for 'Vitai Lampada' by Sir Henry Newbolt; Leslie Norris and Chatto & Windus Ltd for 'Elegy for Lyn James' from *Finding Gold*; the Estate of the late Dr Alfred Noyes and William Blackwood & Sons Ltd for 'Daddy Fell into the Pond' and 'The Highwayman' from *Alfred Noyes: Collected Poems*; Mrs Frances Sommerville for 'A Piper' by Seumas O'Sullivan from *Collected Poems* (Orwell Press, Dublin); Chatto & Windus Ltd and the Executors of the Estate of Wilfred Owen for 'Anthem for Doomed Youth' from *The Collected Poems of Wilfred Owen*, edited by C. Day-Lewis; Penguin Books Ltd for 'Under the Hazy, Blossom-laden Sky' by Okamoto Jun from *The Penguin Book of Japanese Verse*, translated by Geoffrey Bownas and Anthony Thwaite, copyright © Geoffrey Bownas and Anthony Thwaite, 1964; Maeve Peake for 'Sensitive, Seldom and Sad' by Mervyn Peake from *Rhymes Without Reason* (Methuen Children's Books); William Heinemann Ltd for 'The Snitterjipe' by James Reeves from *Prefabulous Animiles*; Richard Rieu for 'The Hippopotamus's Birthday' and 'The Paint Box' by E. V. Rieu from *The Flattered Flying Fish and Other Poems* (Methuen); Michael Rosen for 'I've Had This Shirt' and 'My Brother is Making a Protest about Bread' from *Mind Your Own Business* (Deutsch); R. C. Scriven for 'The Marrog'; Ian Serraillier for 'The Tickle Rhyme' from *The Monster Horse* (O.U.P.) copyright 1950, Ian Serraillier; James MacGibbon as the Executor of the Estate of Stevie Smith for 'Not Waving but Drowning' from *The Collected Poems of Stevie Smith* (Allen Lane); Macmillan, London and Basingstoke, and Mrs Iris Wise for 'The Rivals' from *Collected Poems by James Stephens*; Granada Publishing Ltd for 'A Welsh Testament' from *Tares* by R. S. Thomas, © 1961 R. S. Thomas; Barbara Euphan Todd for 'The Calendar'; George Allen & Unwin (Publishers) Ltd for 'At the Sign of the Prancing Pony' from *The Lord of the Rings*, and 'Chip the Glasses and Crack the Plates' and 'Far Over the Misty Mountains' from *The Hobbit* by J. R. R. Tolkien; Sidgwick & Jackson Ltd for 'Romance' by W. J. Turner; Faber & Faber Ltd for 'Boy at the Window' by Richard Wilbur from *Advice to a Prophet*; Ann Wolfe for 'The Blackbird' by Humbert Wolfe from *Kensington Gardens* (Benn); Martin Secker & Warburg Ltd for 'Hard Frost' by Andrew Young from *Complete Peoms*, edited by Leonard Clark.

Index of First Lines

Index of Authors